## How to Op ncially Successful

Donated to Neva Lomason
Memorial Library

by the Rotary Club of
Carrollton and the Rotary
Foundation

through the Friends of the
Library Matching Gift
Program

2011

# Ca iling

# ess:

### With Companion CD-ROM

D1259994

## Eileen Figure Sandlin

With Foreword By RL "Bud" Abraham,
president of Detail Plus Car Appearance Systems

**WEST GA REG LIB SYS**
**Neva Lomason**
**Memorial Library**

# HOW TO OPEN & OPERATE A FINANCIALLY SUCCESSFUL CAR DETAILING BUSINESS: WITH COMPANION CD-ROM

Copyright © 2011 Atlantic Publishing Group, Inc.
1405 SW 6th Avenue • Ocala, Florida 34471 • Phone 800-814-1132 • Fax 352-622-1875
Web site: www.atlantic-pub.com • E-mail: sales@atlantic-pub.com
SAN Number: 268-1250

No part of this publication may be reproduced, stored in a retrieval system, or transmitted in any form or by any means, electronic, mechanical, photocopying, recording, scanning, or otherwise, except as permitted under Section 107 or 108 of the 1976 United States Copyright Act, without the prior written permission of the Publisher. Requests to the Publisher for permission should be sent to Atlantic Publishing Group, Inc., 1405 SW 6th Avenue, Ocala, Florida 34471.

Library of Congress Cataloging-in-Publication Data

Sandlin, Eileen Figure.
  How to open & operate a financially successful car detailing business : with companion CD-ROM / by Eileen Figure Sandlin.
    p. cm.
  Includes bibliographical references and index.
  ISBN-13: 978-1-60138-279-5 (alk. paper)
  ISBN-10: 1-60138-279-0 (alk. paper)
  1.  Automobile detailing. 2.  New business enterprises--Management. I. Title. II. Title: How to open and operate a financially successful car detailing business.
  TL152.15.S26 2010
  629.28'72--dc22
                        2010004187

All trademarks, trade names, or logos mentioned or used are the property of their respective owners and are used only to directly describe the products being provided. Every effort has been made to properly capitalize, punctuate, identify and attribute trademarks and trade names to their respective owners, including the use of ® and ™ wherever possible and practical. Atlantic Publishing Group, Inc. is not a partner, affiliate, or licensee with the holders of said trademarks.

**LIMIT OF LIABILITY/DISCLAIMER OF WARRANTY:** The publisher and the author make no representations or warranties with respect to the accuracy or completeness of the contents of this work and specifically disclaim all warranties, including without limitation warranties of fitness for a particular purpose. No warranty may be created or extended by sales or promotional materials. The advice and strategies contained herein may not be suitable for every situation. This work is sold with the understanding that the publisher is not engaged in rendering legal, accounting, or other professional services. If professional assistance is required, the services of a competent professional should be sought. Neither the publisher nor the author shall be liable for damages arising herefrom. The fact that an organization or Web site is referred to in this work as a citation and/or a potential source of further information does not mean that the author or the publisher endorses the information the organization or Web site may provide or recommendations it may make. Further, readers should be aware that Internet Web sites listed in this work may have changed or disappeared between when this work was written and when it is read.

PROJECT MANAGER: Erin Everhart • PEER REVIEWER: Marilee Griffin
PRE-PRESS & PRODUCTION DESIGN: Holly Marie Gibbs • INTERIOR DESIGN: Samantha Martin
FRONT COVER DESIGN: Meg Buchner • meg@megbuchner.com
BACK COVER DESIGN: Jackie Miller • millerjackiej@gmail.com

Printed in the United States                    Printed on Recycled Paper

We recently lost our beloved pet "Bear," who was not only our best and dearest friend but also the "Vice President of Sunshine" here at Atlantic Publishing. He did not receive a salary but worked tirelessly 24 hours a day to please his parents. Bear was a rescue dog that turned around and showered myself, my wife, Sherri, his grand-  parents Jean, Bob, and Nancy, and every person and animal he met (maybe not rabbits) with friendship and love. He made a lot of people smile every day.

We wanted you to know that a portion of the profits of this book will be donated to The Humane Society of the United States. *—Douglas & Sherri Brown*

---

The human-animal bond is as old as human history. We cherish our animal companions for their unconditional affection and acceptance. We feel a thrill when we glimpse wild creatures in their natural habitat or in our own backyard.

Unfortunately, the human-animal bond has at times been weakened. Humans have exploited some animal species to the point of extinction.

The Humane Society of the United States makes a difference in the lives of animals here at home and worldwide. The HSUS is dedicated to creating a world where our relationship with animals is guided by compassion. We seek a truly humane society in which animals are respected for their intrinsic value, and where the human-animal bond is strong.

Want to help animals? We have plenty of suggestions. Adopt a pet from a local shelter, join The Humane Society and be a part of our work to help companion animals and wildlife. You will be funding our educational, legislative, investigative and outreach projects in the U.S. and across the globe.

Or perhaps you'd like to make a memorial donation in honor of a pet, friend or relative? You can through our Kindred Spirits program. And if you'd like to contribute in a more structured way, our Planned Giving Office has suggestions about estate planning, annuities, and even gifts of stock that avoid capital gains taxes.

Maybe you have land that you would like to preserve as a lasting habitat for wildlife. Our Wildlife Land Trust can help you. Perhaps the land you want to share is a backyard— that's enough. Our Urban Wildlife Sanctuary Program will show you how to create a habitat for your wild neighbors.

So you see, it's easy to help animals. And The HSUS is here to help.

2100 L Street NW • Washington, DC 20037 • 202-452-1100
www.hsus.org

# Dedication

*To Edward and Eleanore Figure*
*Your boundless love and support make my heart soar.*

# Table of Contents

# Chapter 3:
## Test Driving Your Market                                    53

# Chapter 4:
## Legal and Administrative Details                            69

# Chapter 5:
## Mapping Out the Business                                    87

# Chapter 6:
# Setting Up Shop                99

# Chapter 7:
# Car Love                         115

# Chapter 8:
# Buffer Zone                      127

# Chapter 9:
# Your Pit and Polish Crew         143

# Chapter 10:
## Owner's Guide to Advertising                    161

# Chapter 11:
## Publicity 101 for Fun and Profit                187

# Chapter 12:
# Financing Primer                207

# Chapter 13:
# Approaching the Finish Line        229

# Conclusion:
# Start Your Engines                245

# Appendix A:
# The Sample Business Plan         247

# Appendix B:
# Sample Performance Evaluations
# and Employment Forms            261

## Appendix C:
## Market Research Survey                    267

## Appendix D:
## Resources                                 271

## Glossary of Terms                          277

## Bibliography                              281

## Author Biography                          283

## Index                                     285

# Foreword

For years, auto detailing was nothing more than an automotive car care service done by or for the auto dealer to get used cars ready for resale.

If an individual was doing the work for the dealer, he or she typically did it from a "back-alley" operation that had access to water and could handle a few cars. There was little professionalism about the work, the people, the technology, or the facility itself because the only thing the auto dealer cared about was a cheap price and a fast turn-around to get the vehicle to the lot for resale.

In the late 1970s, we began to see some changes occurring in the U.S. and Canadian market — mainly, the rise in vehicle prices. As prices increased, the financing terms began to increase from the 12- and 24-month contracts of the '70s to the 60- or 84-month contracts today. The average price of a new car in 1978 was $6,379. Today, that price is $27,000. The average length someone owned a vehicle in 1978 about three years. Today, it is reported to be about six years. People are paying more for their vehicles, keeping them longer, and recognizing that they represent a substantial investment, often the second-largest investment next to their house.

Couple this with changes that were occurring in society. More women were working outside the home, and families had more disposable income, but less time. As a result, people became more protective of their leisure time and did not want to spend weekends washing and waxing their cars, cutting their lawn, or cleaning their gutters. They began to seek others to do these things for them. The United States and Canada were moving from a do-it-yourself economy to a more do-it-for-me economy. And in the automatic carwash business, you see a huge proliferation of such facilities springing up all over the country, reflecting the consumer demand for others to take care of their motor vehicles for them.

All of a sudden, auto detailing, which had long been the ugly duckling of the car care industry, was a car care service that motorists were looking for but could not find it because most of the operations focused on providing the work for auto dealers only. Furthermore, typical motorists were not even familiar with the service. They knew they wanted someone to polish and wax their cars, clean and shampoo their interiors, and maybe steam clean the engine, but they were not aware what this was called or where they could get such services done. Many turned to the auto dealer, the gas station, the body shop, and the car wash in search of such a service. And, in most cases, they were rebuked because even these auto care businesses did not provide such services to individuals. However, as motorists became more persistent in their request for the services, automatic car wash businesses realized there was a potential to offer such services to their customers, and that began the retail auto detailing business.

There were some bumps in the road to legitimize auto detailing as a retail service, but by-and-large, car wash businesses began to enjoy excellent revenues by offering detailing to the public. For many, the commitment to providing full-service restoration detailing services was more than they wanted to do, so the car wash industry began to focus on a more simple detail service, what is now known as express maintenance detailing services. Whereas restoration services were performed on older cars in poor condition, maintenance services were performed on new or well-maintained cars in 30 minutes or less. This fit perfectly for the car wash operation, where a customer was already there for ten to 30 minutes.

As the consumer demand for detailing services continued to grow, alert investors began to enter the business, both individuals and franchise-type operations. Not knowing much about the business, many of these early operations failed due to lack of information. This brings us to *How to Open & Operate a Financially Successful Car Detailing Business: With Companion CD-ROM*, a complete resource for anyone wanting to know what it takes to establish a detailing business. The information in this book has been well researched, calling on detailing industry experts from both the supplier and operator level to provide information and insights for the budding entrepreneur. The writing is fun, humorous, and not at all boring, as many how-to books can be. The reader is given a basic, step-by-step primer of the necessary steps to establish a business in general and also the specifics involved in a business that offers detailing services. While this book is not the final answer, it offers the reader more than enough information to get them started and provides excellent sources to find more information on every subject discussed.

As the founder of Detail Plus Car Appearance Systems and a 40-year veteran in the carwash and detail business as an operator, distributor, and manufacturer, I found the information in this book invaluable, and you will, too, in your quest to establish your own detailing business. Even experienced detailers — many of whom do not have a great deal of business savvy — can benefit from reading this book and taking advantage of the resources provided. *How to Open & Operate a Financially Successful Car Detailing Business* is a well-written, easy-to-read, informative publication that anyone involved in or interested in getting into the detailing business should read.

### RL ìBudî Abraham, president

Detail Plus Car Appearance Systems
Portland, Oregon

RL "Bud" Abraham, founder and president of Detail Plus Car Appearance Systems, is a 40-year veteran in the car appearance industry and is considered the top expert in the worldwide car detailing field. He is the founder and executive director of the International Detailing Association, a member of the Western Carwash Association Board of Directors, and has served as a board member for the International Carwash Association on three occasions. He writes regular columns on the subject of auto detailing and appearance care in several major trade journals, and consults on the subjects worldwide.

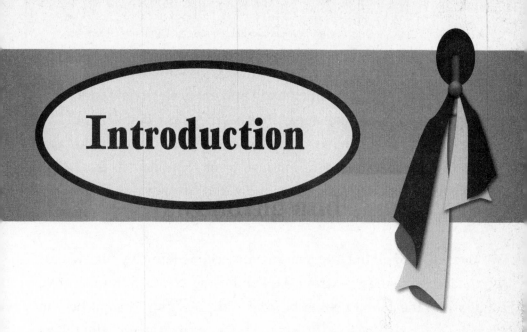

# Introduction

Americans love their cars. They rack up billions of miles on their odometers every year, they deck them out with custom wheels and accessories, and they lovingly pamper them in garages all across the United States so they can show them off in custom car shows or street cruises, or just have them gleaming in their driveway. So it is no surprise this love affair with cars and other vehicles — which has spanned more than 100 years — has spawned a very lucrative, professional car detailing market.

Car detailers do much more than just wash, wax, and clean or shampoo the interior of their vehicles, although those services are certainly at the heart of their job. They also provide a number of specialized services to help restore vehicles to showroom condition. This may include everything from upholstery reconditioning and odor removal, to window tinting, paintless dent repair (PDR), paint protection, carpet dyeing, and much more.

That is where you come in. Because you are reading this book, you are probably a car aficionado and enjoy sleek new cars, family sedans, and vintage autos alike. A career as a detailer could be the dream job you have always wanted and, best of all, you can make plenty of money doing it — a lot of money, in fact. All it takes are good detailing skills and a dose of savvy business acumen to keep the whole operation cranking.

You will find all the information you need to launch your own car detailing business — from the behind-the-scenes administrative work to the actual task of buffing and polishing — right here in *How to Open & Operate a Financially Successful Car Detailing Business*. So let us get our engines roaring.

# Chapter 1

## Detailing 101: Business Basics

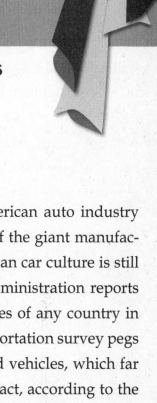

Despite the huge upheaval in the American auto industry in 2009 because of the bankruptcies of the giant manufacturers General Motors and Chrysler, American car culture is still very much alive. The Federal Highway Administration reports that the U.S. has the most passenger vehicles of any country in the world. A 2006 U.S. Department of Transportation survey pegs that number at nearly 251 million registered vehicles, which far exceeds the number of licensed drivers. In fact, according to the U.S. Census Bureau POPClock, the population of the entire country was more than 308 million in late 2009, so in essence there is more than ⅘ of a vehicle for every person — babies, toddlers, and children, too — in our land.

Here is another interesting statistic: A study by the National Automobile Dealers Association indicates that the average age of the cars in operation in 2007 — the latest year for which statistics are available — was 9.2 years, while the average age of light trucks was 7.1 years. People are holding on to their cars longer for many reasons, the biggest of which might be the unstable economy. And as vehicle quality improves, so does life expectancy. The escalating cost of cars and other vehicles also undoubtedly plays a role in the public's decision to drive the wheels off their wheels.

What all this means for you, the aspiring car detailer, is that you will have many opportunities to bathe, buff, polish, restore, and otherwise pamper those vehicles to make them look like new again. If history is any indication, Americans' love for their cars will not be dimmed by encroaching age. If anything, car buffs and ordinary folks alike should be more interested than ever in the restorative services you will provide as a car detailer.

Detailing as a profession has been around for only a few decades, but the concept actually was conceived in 1901 when furniture polish maker Frank Meguiar Jr. realized that the excellent wood polish he mixed with an eggbeater also could be applied to the sides of the wooden horseless carriages produced by Ransom Olds and Henry Ford. Until the 1940s, however, only the wealthiest citizens had the means to have their vehicles detailed. After World War II, auto dealers realized that a little spit and polish could make used vehicles look new and exciting again, and they started adding full-service detailing departments to their establishments.

While detailing pretty much always has had a place in car culture, the profession experienced a renaissance toward the end of the 20th century, no doubt because of the tendency of car owners to keep their vehicles longer. Back in 1969, the median age for cars was 5.1 years. As the average age has increased, so has the demand for auto-detailing services — as well as the need for new detailers to handle all that business.

If you have ever painstakingly washed and waxed your car (by hand, of course), then you already have the basic skills needed to be a detailer. But as mentioned earlier, there is much more to detailing than cleaning, shampooing, and polishing. Other services commonly offered by detailers include PDR, paint touch-up, odor removal, upholstery repair, windshield chip repair, and carpet dyeing.

But before moving on, it is important to note what detailing is not. Detailing in the purest sense does not involve pinstriping a car, adding bodyside moldings, bolting on bike racks, adding fender flares, or applying window graphics; those are customizing services. Detailing refers only to the cleaning and polishing of vehicles. This is not to say you cannot offer customizing services as part of a full-service detailing shop. But, frankly, it is much easier to start a new business that focuses on just a few services rather than to try to be the king — or queen — of automotive services right out of the gearbox. If you try to do too much, you will quickly find yourself overwhelmed and burned out. Instead, start small and aspire to big things later.

## CASE STUDY: A SENSE OF PROFESSIONALISM

RL "Bud" Abraham
Detail Plus Car Appearance Systems Inc.
P.O. Box 20755
Portland, OR 97294
Phone: 503-251-2955, 800-284-0123
(toll free)
Fax: 503-251-5975
E-mail: buda@detailplus.com
Web site: www.detailplus.com

RL "Bud" Abraham has been involved with the car care industry for nearly 40 years. He was the owner of two Detail Plus Detailing Centers in Portland, Oregon, for ten years and is the founder and president of Detail Plus Car Appearance Systems Inc., a leading manufacturer of autodetailing systems and related car-care systems and products. There are more than 25 Detail Plus centers around the world, including locations in the Middle East, eastern and western Europe, Central America, Mexico, and the Mediterranean.

A graduate of the University of Portland with both Bachelor and Master of Arts degrees, Abraham has served the detailing industry in many ways. He was a member on the board of directors for the International Carwash Association and, at press time, was a member of the Western Carwash Association. He is the founding member of the Professional Detailing Association and the International Detailing Association, as well as the first executive director of each organization. He is or has been the detailing editor for several trade journals, including *Professional Carwashing & Detailing, Detailer's Digest,* and *Auto Remarketing* and is a frequent contributor to numerous auto-detailing online forums. He is a frequent speaker at industry trade shows, including Car Care World Expo, Mobile Tech & Detailing Expo, Midwest Carwash Association Expo, and Car Care Expo.

Abraham has witnessed many changes in the world of detailing over four decades, but notes that the industry's basic technology and methodology has remained the same.

"It is still an industry using primitive technology, like heavy electric buffers, shop vacuums, chemicals in plastic bottles, rags, and buckets," he said. "There [continues to be a] general mess and disorganization in shops, which are operated mostly by wanna-be entrepreneurs with no formal training and not much business savvy."

This is one thing Abraham said he would certainly like to see change. He believes the low cost of entry for mobile-detailing operations has contributed to the proliferation of detailing businesses, which is not necessarily a good thing because quality is sometimes sacrificed.

"Overall, this industry has about as much savvy as a shoe-shine business," he said. "It can be entered by almost anyone for a few hundred dollars, so just about anyone can start a business. That's why there are so many fatalities in the industry. It is not uncommon for people to go into and out of business in just a few months."

He also noted that too many part-timers are in the business, working out of their garages or car trunks on weekends just to earn a few extra bucks. Basically, what is lacking is a sense of professionalism, and without it, a new detailing enterprise is doomed to fail. In addition, the industry has lacked strong leadership.

Abraham has developed what he considers to be a fool-proof, step-by-step plan for opening a successful detailing shop. The steps in the plan include:

1. Determine from an objective point of view whether there is a market for a detailing business in your area, and determine where it is.

2. Figure out approximately how much it will cost to set up and maintain a detailing business that has enough operating capital to sustain the business and you until it can sustain itself.

3. Figure out where you will get this money. Without operating capital, a business will fail. The SBA says the reason why two out of three small businesses fail is because of a lack of sufficient operating

capital. This applies to detailing shops, as well. You simply need to have the money.

4.  Know how to use the money you do obtain to operate the business wisely.

5.  Take some classes in operating a business, or better yet, find a mentor to help you learn how to set up and operate a business.

6.  Write a business plan that will tell you how to set up the business, where the markets are, how you are going to get business, and how you will advertise and promote the business.

7.  Establish a budget based on projected sales and the expenses you will incur operating the business.

Abraham said another reason why detailing businesses fail is because they often are owned by technicians who do not understand how to operate a business. When they are confronted with management, financial, and administrative problems, they may try to solve the problems using their technical knowledge — or they may do nothing at all. In either case, they will fail.

Abraham is not a big fan of the mobile-detailing companies, as some do not realize detailing is not different from other auto-service providers, such as car washes, lube and oil shops, tire stores, muffler shops, and auto-repair shops. When starting out in detailing, your capital is crunched, so some think that by avoiding the overhead costs of brick-and-mortar, they are saving in the long run. But mobile detailers work long hours, accounting in a bottom-line hourly wage with no vacation, sick leave, or health insurance.

"They [also] waste huge amounts of good detailing time driving from here to there for customers, charging less than a fixed location for their services," he said. "The current cost of gasoline is causing many of the smarter mobile detailers to reconsider their business model because they simply cannot make any money when the price per gallon for gasoline goes up $4 or more. Overall, this is not the way a professional wants the business to run in the long run."

When it comes to finding a proper brick-and-mortar location, Abraham stressed that it is important to do your homework and home in on your target market.

"For example, if you are targeting auto dealers, then you need to locate in an area where there are numerous auto dealerships — and preferably new car dealerships, because they are more stable and do not go out of business the way many used car dealers do," he said. "If you are targeting consumers, you obviously want to target those with disposal income and the desire to have someone take care of their vehicles for them. That would be a higher-end residential area or, better yet, the downtown business district where all of these types of people work."

When choosing the proper layout for a new brick-and-mortar building, Abraham noted it must be laid out to allow proper vehicle flow in and out. Normally, you will need enough space for three to four cars, plus a wash bay with proper water-discharge connections tied into the sanitary sewer and capped with an oil/water separator. The facility's appearance is also important. The building must be kept in good repair, and its windows must be clean. The landscaping also must be taken care of regularly. This is the best way to make sure your shop looks like any other legitimate auto-service business.

"You are selling 'clean,' so your business must be that way, too," Abraham said emphatically.

Although you can start a detailing shop anywhere in the country, some areas are more favorable as a result of climate and weather conditions, with southern California, south Florida, and Phoenix, Arizona, currently being top detail markets. Of course, even if you decide to open a detail shop in a good location, you will face challenges and pitfalls just as with any other business.

"Sometimes detailers don't have sufficient money, and they have absolutely no business sense," Abraham said. "They want to be entrepreneurs and think that because they know how to detail and have a few hundred dollars, they can operate a detailing business. But as with any business, you need knowledge, training, money, and business expertise."

A certain amount of equipment is mandatory to make a detailing business work. But Abraham says some detailers try get started on the cheap, which results in a less-than-successful business operation. This is why Abraham's company, Detail Plus Care Appearance Systems, sells a system that organizes equipment and chemicals to make a detail shop efficient and effective.

"In our shop, the detailer has a work station that supplies all the chemicals and has a built-in vacuum, built-in carpet steam cleaner, and air lines to blow out interiors, and power air tools for buffing, waxing, and shampooing," he said. "These tools are lightweight, easier to use, and more versatile than heavy electric buffers, which are too large for shampooing or applying wax."

Abraham says he has certainly learned a few things over the years about the detailing business, and he offers training and consulting through his company. Some of the wisdom he dispenses to new detailers includes working with your accountant to establish an hourly rate for your services based on your projected monthly expenses and what you have to earn per hour to cover those expenses. Then, estimate the time it takes to do the job to arrive at a price.

"If the market will pay more, certainly you can charge more, but never less," he said.

He also suggests offering packages such as wash and wax, complete exterior detail, complete interior detail, exterior/interior detail, and complete detail. Abraham also emphasized the importance of good management, noting there are three areas of management that detailers must concern themselves with when setting up and operating a business:

1. **People management:** You must have a strategy for handling customers and a selective hiring program; a training program; and a follow-up program for constant retraining and monitoring.

2. **Financial management:** You must adhere to a financial-management program established by your accountant that determines the percentage of sales you should allocate to each expense area.

3. **Equipment/supplies/chemical management:** You need a maintenance and inventory control system so equipment is constantly

maintained, and supply and chemical inventories are controlled and reordered well in advance so they never run out.

In addition, Abraham emphasized the need to keep your business visible in the community in which you work.

"Public relations and community relations are free, but don't just do something," he said. "Develop a plan for keeping your name in the public eye by highlighting interesting things your company does. For example, allow the local cheerleading squad to hold a charity car wash at your detailing shop, or to sell car wash or detailing tickets to raise money. Let them keep a certain percentage of every ticket they sell, and keep the rest as profit for your business. Or try a cross-promotion with another business. The opportunities are limitless."

According to Abraham, the best customer is the one you can get for the least amount of time, money, and effort. This is why he said that if you have done everything else right, you may never have to spend a lot of money on paid advertising. But if you do advertise, remember that detailing services are not all you are selling. You also are selling investment protection, leisure time freedom, and ego gratification. It is a potent mix, and one that can help make your business quite successful in the long run.

# Ways to Break In

One of the really great benefits in doing car detailing as a profession is that there are so many ways to enter the field successfully. They include:

**Starting an independent shop:** This is the most expensive way to start a detailing business because it entails buying or leasing a building, outfitting it with the equipment and tools of the trade, and hiring employees to work for you. It is also the most labor-intensive operation because in addition to detailing cars, you have to oversee your employees and manage all the day-to-day tasks of running a small business. If you are detail-oriented (no pun intended), well organized, and energetic, this could be the option for you.

**Starting an express service:** This type of business has a lot in common with a car wash. The customer drives up, and you wash the car, clean the interior, and perform other minor detailing services on request while the customer waits. Express detailing services take only about 30 minutes, and considering that the average charge for a basic wash alone is about $40 to $50, you can make a lot of money by moving cars through quickly.

**Setting up a home-based detailing business:** You will definitely save a lot on overhead by setting up your shop in your garage. By slashing the typical costs of a brick-and-mortar shop from your start-up budget, you will start to make money faster. Be sure to check the zoning restrictions in your neighborhood to make sure you can run a commercial business in a residential neighborhood, and also check with your spouse or partner on this one because once you set up your detailing stations, you may never be able to park your own car in the garage again. Water containment is also a must, as it is illegal by federal and state standards to discharge water on the ground or into a sanitary sewer.

**Buying a franchise:** Franchises are turnkey operations that — for the most part — are ready to go right out of the box. After paying the franchise fee, you are entitled to use the franchisor's proven methods to develop the business. This cuts out a lot of the learning curve you normally would go through as an independent entrepreneur. In addition, the franchisor usually provides business support, training, advertising, and marketing assistance. Finally, you will benefit from the franchise's name recognition, which can be helpful for an otherwise unknown start-up operation.

Franchises are a great way to fast track your entry into the detailing profession. But the conveniences they offer do not come cheap; some franchises can have an initial investment fee of up to $120,000. Nevertheless, you might want to investigate this option. A few franchises you can check out include: Drive-N-Style, a mobile detailing business (**www.drivenstyle.com**); ProntoWash, a hand car-wash business rendered at commercial properties (**www.prontowash.com**); Detail King (**www.detailking.com**), which offers a licensee program that has many of the same benefits of a franchise; and Detail Plus, a leader in the cosmetic car care industry (**www.detailplus.com**).

**Taking over an existing business:** Purchasing an existing detailing business can save you a lot of time and labor. But exercise caution when considering the purchase. Do some research to determine exactly why the owner is selling and whether poor location, reputation, management, or other factors had any bearing on his or her decision to sell. You also will want to have an accountant review the shop's books, sales projections, and monthly expenses to get a good idea of how well the shop performs on a month-to-month basis. Finally, inspect the equipment. The older the business, the older the equipment is likely to be, and if you are trying to buy an existing shop as a turnkey venture, you do not want to have to replace a lot of outdated equipment.

**Working on site at a car wash:** It is very common for car washes to offer detailing as one of their services. So you can try arranging a deal where you do the detailing at the car wash. As part of the deal, try to negotiate free workspace and give the car-wash owner a set percentage of each detailing fee. That is usually a more cost-effective way to compensate the owner than paying a rental fee.

**Contracting services to auto dealers:** No matter how poorly the auto market is doing, auto dealers always need someone to detail used cars before selling. You may be able to build a nice stable of auto-dealer clients simply by approaching them with a professional proposal to provide services.

**Servicing commercial, fleet, and car-rental accounts:** You can make plenty of money in this arena, but competition is fierce. Because it will take time to set up these types of accounts, it is probably better to start off detailing everyday passenger vehicles, but pursuing commercial clients always should be part of your future game plan.

**Providing mobile detail services:** This is the more affordable alternative to having your own brick-and-mortar shop. Mobile detailers offer professional services to clients right at their home or office. Depending on the zoning in your community and the willingness of the landlord, it also may be possible to set up shop under a canopy in the parking lot of an office building or big-box retailer. Mobile detailers must bring all their own equipment along with them — as well as enough onboard water to wash those dirty cars — so you will have environmental issues to consider. But mobile detailing is a viable option that puts you on the road to a quick start-up.

## Assessing the competition

Because it is possible to start a car detailing business with a low initial investment, a lot of people enter the field with little more than a shop vacuum and buffer. But those folks are not your real competition as a professional auto detailer; rather, your serious competition will include:

- **Brick-and-mortar detailing shops:** Naturally, these detailers are the most visible in the market, but they also are likely to charge the most because of their overhead costs. Pick a market that is not in direct competition with the established detail shops, then price your services competitively to attract some of the same business.

- **Mobile detailers:** Detailers on wheels can go anywhere in the market, so no matter where you are set up, crossing paths with competitors is likely. By running the most professional operation possible, you can set yourself apart from the merely adequate businesses. Although you do have to purchase a lot of equipment and possibly a vehicle to run a mobile business, the potential profits are rewarding.

- **Car washes:** Car washes tend to offer express maintenance detail services to their customers. That opens the door for your full-service operation.

- **DIYers:** Yes, the weekend warriors who like to wash and polish up their rides must be considered competition, too. It will be your job to persuade them to leave the buffing to you so they can spend their free time on other pursuits.

# Earning Potential

While it is believed that about 15,000 independent car detailers are hard at work in the United States, what is not readily apparent is how much they earn. This is partly because the price of detailing services varies widely by region, and partly because detailers can be found everywhere from standalone businesses to auto dealerships.

For example, the Bureau of Labor Statistics, which lumps car detailers into its "Cleaners of Vehicles and Equipment" category, states that the median hourly wage for such workers is $11.67 an hour. On the other hand, *Professional Carwashing & Detailing* magazine says that detailers can earn up to $75 an hour.

A better way to estimate your potential earnings is to consider how much you can charge for detailing services. According to Detail King, a detailer should be able to earn nearly $100 a day by washing and waxing just two cars — something a one-person operation can accomplish.

Provide basic interior cleaning services on the same two cars, and Detail King says another $80 a day in earnings is possible. *Entrepreneur* magazine reports that a mobile detailing business has the potential to turn an average profit of $100,000 a year.

On the other hand, detailing expert RL "Bud" Abraham of Detail Plus Car Appearance Systems says the figure is closer to $48,000 to $60,000 for most. Either way, this type of business is definitely viable.

A detailer with, say, three employees, should be able to handle as many as eight basic wash-and-wax jobs per day. The following chart shows the math of how much a one-person operation should be able to earn in a day by washing, waxing, and cleaning two to three vehicles, versus how much is possible if the business has employees who can handle up to eight vehicles a day:

| ONE-PERSON OPERATION: DAILY | | |
| --- | --- | --- |
| Number of cars detailed | Projected earnings for wash/wax only | Projected earnings for wash/wax/interior cleaning |
| 2 per day | $100 | $180 |
| 3 per day | $150 | $270 |
| 8 per day | $400 | $720 |

Based on a 260-day year (five days a week x 52 weeks), a detailer could earn:

| ONE-PERSON OPERATION: YEARLY | | |
| --- | --- | --- |
| Number of cars detailed | Projected earnings for wash/wax only | Projected earnings for wash/wax/interior cleaning |
| 2 per day | $26,000 | $46,800 |
| 3 per day | $39,000 | $70,200 |
| 8 per day | $104,000 | $187,200 |

And that is just for the most basic services. Add in premium services such as vinyl and leather repair, as well as higher detailing costs for larger vehicles such as SUVs and trucks, and your earnings will increase. In fact, according to Detail King, the average cost of a detail job that includes exterior machine polishing and full interior detailing is $125 *per vehicle*, although an unscientific survey of the Internet indicated that many detailers charge $200 or more.

A complete detailing job from hood to trunk easily can run $250 to $300 per vehicle or more, depending on your ZIP code. Sell a few of those packages over and above the basic services outlined above, and your gross sales will really grow. Target people with more disposable income in more affluent areas, and you will do even better.

Auto-detailing experts stress that making more money in this business is not about manically detailing an endless stream of cars; it is about selling other services to customers who are already right there in your clutches and are therefore open to suggestion. The retail term for this is "up-selling," and it is easy to do. Fast-food restaurants have the technique down pat — their clerks are trained to ask whether you would like to "supersize" your meal, or add cookies or a drink to your sandwich order.

You can do the same thing with detailing customers. Suggest to your basic wash-and-wax customer that her leather seats would really look great with a quick application of the conditioning product you carry. Or mention to your full-service detailing customer that window tinting would protect his vehicle's carpets and seats from fading.

The list is endless, but keep in mind that you should sell to the needs of each specific car. The bottom line: No one can really tell you how much you, personally, can earn as a car detailer. It all comes down your dedication and enthusiasm, minus the cost of your detailing products and other operating expenses.

# Chapter 2

**Putting Your Business Into Gear**

# Types of Detailers

Decisions, decisions: Every entrepreneur faces important choices when setting up a lucrative and well-oiled business machine. As a fledgling car detailer, one of the first decisions to make relates to the types of services you will offer, as well as how to bundle those services into packages that will increase the price point of every sale.

## The full-service shop

To start the process, consider the level of service you wish to offer. If you are planning to open a stand-alone business, you probably will choose to be a full-service detailer who offers basic services (washing, waxing, and upholstery care), specialized services (water spot removal and carpet dyeing), and more advanced services (windshield chip repair and gold plating). A full-service shop is the type of business where customers leave their vehicle for several hours. It is customary for detailers to offer complimentary pick-up-and-delivery service for customers who are paying for the works.

Full-service customers include car buffs who do not have time to do their own detailing; those who want to give their beater a face-lift before selling it; people who want to restore a used car to showroom condition; lease customers who are getting ready to turn in their vehicles; folks who want to give their autos a spring spruce-up; and those who wish to prep their cars for winter.

## The express-detailing operation

While an express detailer may offer many of the same services as a full-service dealer, the express detailer focuses on tasks that can be completed in about 15 to 30 minutes per vehicle — hence the name "express." Express detailing is meant to be a vehicle maintenance program and usually targets customers who do not need full-service detailing but want their rides well cared for. For this reason, an express detailer should expect to wash, wax, and vacuum *a lot* of cars. While express detailers can have stand-alone operations, it is more common to find them on site in related businesses such as car washes.

## The mobile-detailing business

A mobile detailer transports all his or her equipment right to the customer in a specially equipped pick-up or van and can provide virtually all the same services of a full-service shop, including upholstery repairs, paint touch-up, and windshield chip repair. Mobile customers usually are interested in regular care and maintenance for their wheels but do not have time to make an appointment to bring the car in. Those interested in spring cleanup and winterizing services also may be customers.

A mobile business offers detailers several benefits to the owner that a stand-alone shop does not. To begin with, mobile businesses offer a full slate of services without the overhead of a brick-and-mortar building. Second, you can service cars pretty much anywhere, from a customer's driveway to the parking lot outside his or her office building, as long as the wastewater is properly contained. Third, a mobile vehicle is like a billboard on wheels, with free exposure to new clients everywhere you go. Put your phone number on the side of the vehicle, and you will likely get calls from people who have seen you tooling around town on your way to jobs. Finally, you can detail entire fleets of vehicles — such as at an auto dealership — right on site.

## Other business options

While it is common to establish one of the three types of businesses mentioned here, you also can mix up all these services as a way to maximize your profits. Detailing purists say this dilutes the business, but face it: The idea here is to make money, and if you have the money and the personnel to diversify, then you can go for it.

# Detailing Basics

The basic exterior express maintenance services include:

- Washing the vehicle by hand
- Using a clay bar to remove stubborn surface contaminants such as industrial fallout, overspray, and rail dust

- Drying the vehicle by hand
- Applying wax or sealants
- Cleaning windows and mirrors
- Applying tire and trim products (dressing)

The basic interior express services include:

- Vacuuming the floor and seats
- Shampooing or steam cleaning the floor, seats, and floor mats
- Cleaning and conditioning leather seats, or cleaning and dressing vinyl seats
- Cleaning and dressing hard surfaces such as the dashboard, door panels, and console
- Cleaning other factory-installed equipment such as vents, knobs, pedals, ashtray, and door jams
- Cleaning windows and the rearview mirror

The complete detail includes one additional service: engine detailing. You will need to invest in a pressure washer to degrease engines, after which you will dress them with water-based products to make them look like new. With a full-service shop or mobile detailing service, you will be able to offer a lot of additional services that can really help improve your bottom line. Among these are:

**Black plastic trim restoration:** A process to restore the luster to exterior plastic, rubber, and vinyl parts, though few perform this service.

**Carpeting and upholstery repair and dyeing:** Eradicating or fixing damage such as cigarette burns, tears, scuffs, and fading from the sun.

**Custom paint touch-up:** Filling in scratches, chips, dings, and other road damage with custom-mixed paint to match the vehicle's original paint job.

**Convertible and ragtop repair:** Everything from replacing the motor, worn-out frame components, and burned stitching to repairing wear spots and frayed areas.

**Gold plating:** Adding a gold touch to the trim, exterior accessories, and auto emblems.

**Headlight renewal:** Removing yellow discoloration and eliminating fogginess.

**Overspray treatment removal:** Fixing the damage from airborne contaminants such as cement and concrete, chemical fallout, environmental fallout, hydrocarbons, iron oxides, and rail dust. This is an excellent service to offer if you are located near an airport, factory, or large industrialized urban area.

**Ozone odor elimination and deodorizing:** Using an ozone generator to remove stubborn odors from cigarettes, pets, mold, mildew, and other sources after you have thoroughly cleaned the interior.

**Paintless dent repair (PDR):** A quick and easy process (once learned) for removing small dents and dings.

**Paint sealer application:** Reapplying the clear coat that makes a vehicle look shiny and new.

**Scotchgard™ application:** Sealing upholstery to prevent soiling and repel stains.

**Teflon® sealant:** A product used on the exterior of vehicles that is superior to wax because it seals paint against rust, oxidation, and other contaminants for a longer period of time.

**Trim and instrumentation repair:** Replacing or repairing the knobs and trim that can get damaged through normal wear-and-tear.

**Vinyl and leather repair:** Repairing tears, cracks, burns, and sun-faded areas.

**Water spot removal:** Removing microscopic pollutants in water that can damage a vehicle's finish.

**Windshield repair:** A quick, convenient injector process in demand by retail customers, insurance companies, rental car agencies, and used car dealers.

**Windshield tinting:** Shielding out damaging UVA and UVB rays that can discolor upholstery.

**Windshield wiper replacement:** A simple process with a high markup and instant profit.

Naturally, some of these services, including PDR, require a little hands-on training before you attempt them on clients' vehicles.

Many of the companies that supply the needed products and tools can help you learn the ropes. For example, Detail Plus Car Appearance Systems (**www.detailplus.com**), an Oregon-based detailing supply company, includes a how-to video along with the tools and accessories you will need to become a PDR master and can provide optional personalized training at an additional cost.

## Bundling your services

Although no detailer worth his or her vehicle wax would turn down a customer who asks for just a single service such as a basic car wash or an ozone odor treatment — you should have an à la carte menu for that purpose — up-selling is the name of the game in the detailing world. For this reason, you need to create a variety of detailing packages to tempt people to spend a little more when they come in or you go to them.

Get creative when dreaming up the detailing packages that will attract the most customers. If your area has a thriving car culture, for example, you could market a custom detail or a new car protection package. An odor elimination package definitely would turn noses — uh, heads — in humid climates. And do not forget spring cleaning and winterizing, packages tied to local events (such as an Indy 500 weekend package), and midweek specials to drive in business on your slower days.

# Cashing In

A casual and unscientific Internet survey of detailing prices in late 2009 indicates that a typical entry-level, complete detailing package as described earlier will run from $100 to as much as

$200, depending on location. You definitely can expect to charge more in large urban areas such as Los Angeles or Miami, and considerably less in Wyoming or Idaho, where the cost of living is lower. On the express detail side, Detail King says interior detailing services typically run $15 to $30 per service. If you have the personnel and space, you should always use an express detailing job as a springboard to landing complete detailing and special services work in the future.

When it comes to those special services, here is a general idea of what detailers are charging for some of the most requested extra services:

- Decal and sticker removal: $30 and up
- Carpet dyeing: $25 per section and up
- Cigarette burn repairs: $25 and up
- Custom paint touch-up: $70 and up
- Scotchgard™ application: $40 and up
- Odor elimination: $40 and up
- Paintless dent repair (PDR): starting at $70 for a single ding
- Vinyl and leather repair: $100 per hour on average
- Windshield repair: $45 and up (or $0 for the customer if an insurance company is picking up the whole tab and will pay you directly)
- Window tinting: $250 and up
- Headlight restoration: $40 per light and up

Before setting your fees, you need to determine your hourly rate. Do a quick survey either by phone or Internet of what the competition in your market area is charging, and price accordingly. If your prices are too high, customers will drive away in droves;

if they are too low, customers may think your services are not good enough to charge more. Whatever you do, do not undersell your efforts. It takes about three to five hours to do a complete detailing, and it is hard work, so do not shortchange yourself on the fee.

There is a more scientific way to set prices than just seeing what the competition is doing. Oregon detailing expert Bud Abraham says you should start by figuring out the true cost of labor and expenses needed to complete a detailing job. You can do this by tallying up the hourly wage, benefits, taxes, workers' comp rates, uniform cost, and so on for the employee (that includes you) who will do the detailing work. Once you have a figure, multiply it by the number of hours it takes to complete a detailing job to come to an equitable price. Abraham says the way to make real money is to improve the "turn rate," or the length of time it takes to detail a vehicle. Others recommend adding 20 percent to the bottom-line figure to work a profit margin into the equation.

# The Underside of Detailing

Although stocking your business with power tools and state-of-the-art products is probably high on your priority list, it is also important to note that you are now a small-business owner. Along with that lofty designation comes a lot of other responsibilities because the business will not run itself while you meticulously run your buffers and sanders over clients' spoilers and rocker panels. Here is a rundown of the various types of tasks you can expect to undertake as the owner of a car detailing business:

## General office duties

- Answering the phone and booking appointments
- Opening the mail
- Talking to product and equipment vendors
- Purchasing detailing supplies for business use
- Purchasing detailing products for resale to clients
- Updating and managing your Web site
- Answering e-mail and blogging
- Invoicing corporate clients
- Paying suppliers and other bills
- Balancing the books (if you do not have an accountant yet) and making estimated tax payments
- Implementing advertising and marketing plans to spread the word about your business
- Networking to make contacts with people who might later use your business or recommend you to others who need detailing services

## Personnel management

- Managing employees' schedules
- Training new employees and updating skills
- Processing the payroll
- Refereeing when disagreements arise

## Front-desk management (site-based only)

- Greeting the public
- Providing excellent customer service and troubleshooting problems
- Running the cash register

- Processing credit cards
- Making bank deposits

**Miscellaneous tasks (site-based only)**

- Keeping the shop, waiting area, and restrooms sparkling clean
- Stocking the shelves with new products and turning older inventory

This might sound like a lot more work than you signed up for, but each of these tasks are essential in running a successful business. But never fear: When you launch your business, the amount of time you will spend on these chores will be minimal because, quite frankly, you will not have a ton of work right out of the gate. As your detailing workload increases, you may find you need help in the form of an administrative assistant or shop manager.

# When the Weather Outside is Frightful

If you are plying your trade as a mobile detailer, you will face some challenges that are not a problem for brick-and-mortar shop owners. Disposing of wastewater is just one of those issues. But trying to make a living when the weather is not cooperating is another problem that can really divert your income stream.

You might try to erect a temporary canopy over your workspace. In theory, that works fine, but what happens if El Niño-produced tornadoes are howling, or a blizzard is roaring in? You will have no choice but to pack up, and face it — no one in his or her right mind is going to be thinking about a clean car at such times, anyway. It would be like taking that $15 car-wash money and tearing it into little pieces for the tornado to carry it away.

The best way you can sidestep the weather is to develop a slate of other services that can augment your normal business. The types of work that detailers commonly pick up during downtimes are windshield chip repair, invisible film protections, and carpet dyeing. You will need a place to do the work, of course, such as a garage. You also will need to drum up some business. These days, one of the fastest ways to contact people is through the social-networking service Twitter (**www.twitter.com**), so make it a priority to start trying to increase your followers as soon as you start accumulating some satisfied customers who might be interested in future detailing specials.

Another possible source of work during inclement weather is the small aircraft and limousine industries. Find a small airport with some nice, dry hangars, or a limo company that parks its vehicles under cover, and pitch your services. Along the same lines, you can offer interior detailing services to boat owners. Work up a special package that will appeal to these customers and offer it on days you are stuck without regular work to do. You could find you are just as busy when the weather is crummy as you are on a sunny day.

Finally, do not overlook the possibilities that go along with your pressure-washing equipment and the chemicals you already have. Use these tools to fill in any income gaps, especially during the winter in northern climes. Some mobile detailers wash and restore lawn furniture, recondition garage floors, or clean and sanitize dog kennels as side jobs during off-peak season. For that matter, when the weather is nice, your pressure-washing equipment would come in handy for power-washing decks, patios, and aluminum siding, too. Because you are carrying everything you need onboard your mobile unit, you can go just about anywhere, anytime and still make a buck.

## CASE STUDY: MANY REVENUE STREAMS

Brandon Conder
Busy B's Mobile Auto Detailing
2515 Glen Meadows
Mesquite, TX 75150
Phone: 214-460-3660
E-mail: busyb321420@yahoo.com
Web site: www.busybs.net

Brandon Conder has been a mobile detailer for more than ten years. His main service area is the Dallas area, but he also drives to cities in neighboring states such as Oklahoma, where he works the Oklahoma State Fair. He also details cars at auto shows.

Auto detailing has been the perfect profession for him because, as he candidly admits, he never liked working for people who would stand over his shoulder and tell him what to do. But while working for bosses like that at a few car washes, he noticed how much business they had. When the opportunity to go mobile presented itself, he leaped at the chance, and a new career was born.

Conder mostly services people who do not have the time to detail their own cars. For some of his older customers, he usually makes house calls so the vehicle owner does not have to do a thing except admire the finished product. Initially, he was most successful advertising his business through newspaper ads and phone books. He did try passing out fliers when he first launched the business but said, "That did not work out quite like I expected, and all I ended up with were blisters on my feet." Eventually, he started using the resources of the Internet instead and stopped all of his print advertising except for an ad in one phone book.

Conder's main workplace may be a detailing trailer, but he has someone capable in charge of all the behind-the-scenes work: his mother. She has kept the business running smoothly over the years, handling taxes and advertising, and covering just about everything else while he stays busy on the job. She also is proficient at talking someone down on a price, which he appreciates because it increases his profit margin. When he first started his business, Conder had five other employees. These days, he needs only one or two people to help him get the job done, which is helpful considering the state of the economy. Even when he works by himself, he can clean a lot of cars. His personal record is 54 cars in a day, which he set when he was working for a used-car dealership.

"On a regular day, it really just depends on the flow as to how many cars I can get done," he said. "Sometimes it is go, go, go, really quick on the outside only; other times, you have to get in there and just mass-overhaul the car. In the case of overhauls, I can only get a handful of those done a day versus the 20 or 30 I can do for simple services."

Thanks to his detailing equipment, Conder has been able to create other lucrative revenue streams.

"I will power-wash anything," he said. "Sometimes the customer wants me to detail and then do the driveway, too. I also have a unit I use to strip stain and clean fences, and that brings me a lot of extra work. Ever since I bought a hot water unit, I have gotten extra jobs just with this piece of equipment."

No matter whether he is detailing or power-washing, Conder always keeps track of his water consumption and runoff, both of which are of interest to environmentalists and the Environmental Protection Agency (EPA). Although the EPA is not likely to swoop in while he is dressing tires, he could be in the crosshairs of municipal officials who could ticket him or turn him in.

"They will actually slap you with a big, fat ticket for power-washing if you don't follow regulations or if they see a bunch of suds and chemicals going down the drain," he said. Usually a mobile-unit owner does not get into trouble unless you make someone mad and that person decides to report you. Then the EPA will come and write you a $1,500 or $2,500 ticket because you are not in compliance. What they say goes. No exceptions."

Tighter clean-water standards are only one way the industry has changed since Conder started his business. He also has noticed a difference in customers.

"People are tighter with their money now," he says. "Sometimes I do more power-washing than car detailing."

Conder uses two to six products on a vehicle.

"The number depends on the customer and what he or she likes," he says. "Some customers don't want anything on their cars. We recently did a big Hummer, and when we were finished, I thought it was still dirty. But the owner did not want any Armor All on the tires or anything else like that. He said he didn't want that greasy, oily stuff on there, and I said that was fine; everyone has a different idea."

But one thing Conder does not use these days is fragrance, because so many people have allergies. But there are other things beside using fragrance — or *not* using fragrance, for that matter — that can be done to make an impression on customers.

"Customers notice just about everything done during a detail," Conder says. "But if the windows sparkle, the tires are dressed, and the rims shine, then the car will look great, and the customer will be happy."

# On Your Mark

As you can see, many opportunities are available for motivated car detailers to make a good living. But before you start dropping cash or flexing your credit muscles to pick up equipment and supplies, take a moment to consider again whether this detailing gig really is the right profession for you. It might sound like a lot of fun to work on cars every day or to clay (use a clay bar to remove imperfections in paint) and polish in the sunshine rather than sitting behind a desk in a stuffy office. But being self-employed takes commitment, motivation, and discipline. You have to be able to focus on and complete even the tasks you dislike, which probably will include the jobs you left on the desk in that stuffy office. You have to be committed to providing excellent customer service, from listening carefully to customers' requirements and needs, to graciously and fairly handling their complaints. You also must treat the business like a profession and not just a hobby that brings in a few extra bucks on the weekend.

Although self-motivation and self-sufficiency are crucial for success, leadership and communication skills are equally as important, especially if you will have employees. Everyone who works for you, from the detailing specialists to the office assistants, will need strong direction, open lines of communication, and fair treatment in order to do their jobs well. And, of course, when they do their jobs well, your own job becomes that much easier — and more enjoyable.

We assume you are up for the challenge. Turn the page to learn how to determine who and where your customers are so you have the best chance of business success.

## Chapter 3

**Test Driving Your Market**

N ow that you have a good idea of the full scope of car detailing, it is time to start thinking about how to actually get customers to use your services. That takes money and targeted advertising, of course. But before you start advertising your business to an unsuspecting public, you have to figure out exactly whom to target. The way to do that is through market research that identifies your target market and the potential buyers within it.

# Driving In Customers Through Market Research

The purpose of market research is two-fold. First, you want to figure out exactly what your potential customers want from a business like yours by looking at what already has been done and how successful it was. Second, you want to figure out whether there is a need for your services in a particular market. That second point cannot be emphasized strongly enough. You can offer the world's best detailing services at the most competitive prices, but if you are trying to sell them in an area where they are just not in demand (the Arctic comes to mind), then all your efforts will be wasted.

There is also the problem of oversaturation. If the area where you want to do business already has several successful detailing companies that have a lock on all the basic wash and wax business, as well as several mobile detailers — and they all have reasonable prices — then it is in your best interest to set your sights on the next community. It will be very tough, if not impossible, to convince other detailers' loyal customers to give you a chance to shine, especially at a higher cost. Likewise, if the area you are interested in is an older community with long-established businesses, your chances of stellar success are probably pretty slim there, too. You are better off looking for a newer area with a greater potential for growth than to try to infiltrate the establishment.

It should be pretty obvious that it is crucial to do this kind of market research before you start dropping cash on your fledgling business. Do not invest in equipment, stock up on detailing products, lease a building, or print advertising materials until you have a sense of whether there is enough business to go around, — or, for that matter, whether the state of the economy will make people more likely to use all their discretionary income on food and prescriptions rather than a great wax job.

Because of their sheer numbers and reach, your strongest competitors are likely to be car washes rather than detailing businesses. In addition to snagging a lot of your prospective exterior washing business, many car washes offer express detailing services, while others provide the full gamut of car-care services. For this reason, as well as because there are few readily accessible detailing statistics available to refer to, it is important to know something about Americans' car-care and car-washing habits.

A 2009 "Elbow Grease Economics" survey conducted by 3M Car Care indicated that Americans are putting more emphasis on car maintenance and appearance because they plan to keep their cars longer. That is good news for someone like you who wants to sell car-care services. Also, the 2008 International Carwash Association's (ICA) "Consumer Car Washing Attitudes and Habits" survey, which is conducted every three years, reports that 65.6 percent of the respondents indicated they use a professional car wash. That is up from 62 percent in 2005. So, it appears that a majority of Americans prefer to use a car wash rather than doing the washing in their own driveways. In fact, ICA says the need for professional car washing actually has risen 10 percent during the past decade.

Armed with this information, your task is to figure out how to compete with the car-wash big boys in your community. Here is how to do it.

## Analyze the demographics

Demographics are not very sexy, and studying them probably does not sound like much fun, but it is actually pretty easy to do. Start by examining all the general research you can get your hands on at no charge — and thanks to the Internet, there is a lot of it. You can access a free key findings fact sheet containing the 2005 ICA data mentioned above, for example, on ICA's Web site (**www.carwash.org**), keywords "Consumer Car Washing Attitudes and Habits." You can order the 2008 data for $75 for non-ICA members at the same site. In addition, many municipalities freely divulge demographic information on their community Web sites. Take Altoona, Pennsylvania, for example. Its community profile at **www.altoona.com** contains information about the population and education levels. Another site called **www.muninetguide.com** turned up Altoona home-value information and links to other statistical research sites. Give this a shot yourself: In a search engine, search the name of each city you are interested in, plus the word "statistics," "community profile," or "demographics" and see what kind of information pops up that can help you determine whether you have chosen a good place to do business. Areas with higher home prices, higher income levels, and a higher concentration of white-collar workers are likely to be good locations for a detailing business.

A couple of valuable tools to check out are the U.S. Census Bureau's *County and City Data Book and Sales and Marketing Management Magazine*, which publishes the "Survey of Buying Power" every September. The *County and City Data Book* offers a real bonanza of demographic information, from the average value of households to the number of people employed in various industries. The "Survey of Buying Power" has total retail sales figures and volumes for different types of businesses, the median age of community residents, and more. You can have your own copy of the data book for $75 or a regional report excerpted from the buying power report for $199 (available at **www.surveyofbuyingpower.com**), but check with your local library first to see whether you can access them for free.

Other sources of demographic information that may be useful are public utilities, which often allow low- or no-cost access to public records; the local chamber of commerce; and the U.S. Census Bureau (**www.census.gov**), which collects plenty of information. Census data, however, may be slightly outdated because it takes a while for the government to collect and publish such a vast amount of information.

Incidentally, a wealth of other interesting car wash and detailing statistics are available if you have the funds. The bad news is that the reports tend to be costly — often $800 and up — and tend to contain way more data than the average detailer needs. But one source worth the money is *Professional Car Washing and Detailing* magazine (**www.carwash.com**), which publishes a "State of the Industry" report in each October issue. Contact the magazine directly to see if you can purchase a back issue or, better yet, subscribe to receive a constant flow of useful news and information. You can get a free introductory subscription when you subscribe online.

With all the demographic statistics floating around, it can get overwhelming sifting through the data. Here are the key demographics that are pertinent to a detailing business:

- **Age:** The ICA says that nearly 63 percent of full-service car-wash customers are aged 50 and above, so it would make sense to find out where the baby boomers live and shop when seeking a market.

- **Gender:** Women are more frequent consumers of car-wash services (roughly 58 percent are women, according to ICA).

- **Income:** The higher the disposable income, the more likely a person is to use a full-service car wash and/or detailing service.

- **Occupation:** As with income, occupation can be an indication of how much disposable income potential customers have. Therefore, a white-collar neighborhood with higher home values could be a good place to establish your business.

- **Education:** Typically, the higher the education, the higher the income, and the better the chance of attracting customers.

Armed with this data, you can make some assumptions about the area you are considering. For example, say you have found an area populated with plenty of white-collar workers with high incomes. That might be a great place to base your business, but if those jobs are concentrated in a particular industry (think automotive or high-tech) and that industry tanks, your business will, too. That is a red flag you cannot ignore.

## Assess the competition

If you want to thrive, you need to know who your competition is and what drives them. Start by assessing your direct competition, which includes the car detailing shops and mobile detailers in the geographical area you are considering. Check out the services they offer, where they are located, and how well they are doing. Do the same thing with the car washes because, even though not all car washes offer detailing services, the ones that do probably will be your strongest competitors. Once again, the Internet can be a great way to gather information, as so many companies have

Web pages. You might also have a look at Reference USA (**www. referenceusa.com**), a searchable database of more than 14 million U.S. companies, to see if any of the larger competitors in your area are listed. Reference USA contains information such as number of employees and sales volume, both of which can be useful for your analysis. The database is accessible through public libraries, so call your local branch to see if it is available there.

In order to make some sense of the data, create a SWOT analysis. This is a strategic-planning tool used in business to assess the competition in terms of:

- Strengths
- Weaknesses
- Opportunities
- Threats

Using a computer spreadsheet or word-processing program, create a two-column, two-row table, then box the cells to create four quadrants. Label each quadrant with one of the SWOT terms, then insert the information you have gathered for your first competitor into the appropriate boxes. Create a similar chart for each of your competitors.

Study the information to determine if there are any patterns you can use to your advantage, such as a weakness each competitor has that you can capitalize on. It is also helpful to create a SWOT analysis for your own business to see how it will stack up against the competition.

Here is what a SWOT analysis for a one-person detailing business might look like:

| STRENGTHS | WEAKNESSES |
|---|---|
| Have sufficient start-up capital to survive a first-year business learning curve | No accounting experience — need help |
| Have been detailing personal vehicles for years, so know the ropes | Lack general business-operating knowledge |
| Motivated and willing to work hard | |
| OPPORTUNITIES | THREATS |
| Local car washes do not offer any detailing services | Economy is still weak in market area |
| No local mobile detailing services in area, either (but see Threats) | Sole mobile detailer in the area failed in first year |
| | Local government may institute new water run-off regulations |

It is important to note that everything presented here is a pretty simplistic way to attack market research. There is way more you can do — as well as way more a true market researcher would recommend — including focus groups and surveys. *You will find a sample market research survey in Appendix C.* Your start-up budget is likely to be stretched tighter than a circus high wire, and you signed up to be a detailer, not a market researcher. But do not worry; the techniques presented here have been simplified so you easily can do some research of your own that will help you get a feel for the depth and breadth of your market. If you find this too time-consuming or too complicated, you might consider hiring a market researcher to assist. Be forewarned: Market research help does not come cheap, but it may be the only way you can get the job done. For leads on a market researcher, check the Yellow Pages or ask the local chamber of commerce or other business organizations for recommendations.

## Create a marketing plan

Armed with all this information, you are ready to put together a marketing plan that will help you decide how to meet and greet the competition — and hold your own among them. The marketing plan does not have to be lengthy or especially detailed, but it does have to contain your strategy for introducing your company to the public and keeping it visible. The good news is that the info in your marketing plan later will become part of your overall business plan, so you will actually be making inroads on that process right now.

Some basic elements your marketing plan should include are:

- A situation analysis, in which you discuss your market, demographics, opportunities, and services. The findings from your SWOT analyses should be presented here.

- A brief discussion of your prospective customers using the information you have already compiled.

- A rundown of your pricing strategies, including how they will compare to the competition and whether you will do any discounting or couponing to attract business.

- A detailed list of marketing strategies based on your findings about your target market, as well as a timeline for implementing them. Those strategies may be anything from an open house and newspaper advertising, to couponing and blogging.

- A discussion of financial objectives, which are the benchmarks you hope to reach in your first year of business.

Once again, this is a simplistic approach to creating a marketing plan, but in general, it is sufficient for most detailing shops.

# Envisioning Your Business Future

When you first conceived the idea for a detailing business, no doubt you had a vision of what the business would be like once it was successful. Maybe you imagined having a detailing superstore with an attached casino and raw bar, or maybe you see yourself as a wealthy absentee owner who directs a chain of shops and an army of detailing experts from behind a curtain in the penthouse at Trump Tower. It is good to have dreams, no matter how pie-in-the-sky, but it is also important to note that business experts say that if you articulate your dreams, you are more likely to achieve them. For this reason, you should write a vision statement for your detailing operation (though you probably should rein in any dreams you have that remotely resemble those mentioned earlier).

In a vision statement, you speculate about where you want to take the business. In a way, it is "brass ring" thinking: identifying exactly what it is you want before you have actually acquired it. For example, a vision statement for a detailer might be something like this: "XYZ Detailing, a full-service enterprise, will become the leader in the metro area by offering more services than the local car washes while using green products not available at any of the express detailers in the area." Becoming the No. 1 detailer may seem like wishful thinking, especially if you are a one-person operation on a shoestring budget. But William Arthur Ward, an inspirational writer, put it this way: "If you can imagine it, you can achieve it. If you can dream it, you can become it." That includes you, so write that vision statement now.

## CASE STUDY: HAVE A VISION

Michael Patrick
Appearance Plus Inc.
1508 S Babcock St
Melbourne, FL 32901
Phone: 321-952-4346

Michael Patrick has been in the auto appearance and reconditioning industry since 1987. He has owned two car washes and seven detail shops in southern California and south Florida and currently works in central Florida. His company specializes in detailing cars, boats, and RVs.

This experienced businessman does much more than just detailing. He also offers service, training, and product distribution. He writes articles for several trade publications, has been listed in *Entrepreneur Magazine*'s "Top 500 Small Business Opportunities," and has been featured on CBS News in a story on headlight restoration. Since 2005, his business has been ranked No. 1 in Brevard County, Florida. In 2006, he won an award that named him the No. 1 paintless dent repair (PDR) person in the world.

Patrick owns two self-serve car washes that offer detailing, tinting, paint and dent repair services, headlight restoration, bumper repair, and PDR. He also sells truck accessories on premises. He services car dealers, fleets, insurance companies, government agencies, and the public.

Patrick started out as a mobile detailer. As is often the case with mobile detailers, he started detailing as a way to earn extra money but soon expanded his business by adding new services and creating a one-stop-shop automotive experience. As a result, Appearance Plus is now a multimillion-dollar business with locations in nearly every state and 45 foreign countries.

"My business succeeded because I had a vision of what this could be after having some success early on," he said. "Working hard every day and having a plan made all the difference. Not many people knew what detailing was in the 1980s, but now it is a household name, which makes competition among detailers stiffer. At the same time, detailing products and equipment are much better, and the market is larger, so there are definitely good opportunities for new detailers today."

But the road to detailing success was not without bumps. One major obstacle Patrick had to overcome was a lack of cash to do the things he wanted to do fast enough. As a result of hard work, he was able to save a portion of his profits, which ultimately allowed him to upgrade his equipment and services on an ongoing basis. Another important thing he lacked in his formative years was a mentor, he says. He said he feels he might have been more successful faster if he had an experienced detailer acquaintance whom he could count on for advice and support. Because of that, Patrick is doing his part today to help other fledgling business owners by consulting with and advising hundreds of detailers worldwide.

One of the first steps Patrick said is necessary when establishing a new detail shop is to promote it well. He recommends creating marketing fliers and business cards, then completely blanketing the area where the business is located. He also emphasized that completing work on time, doing a good job, and being fairly priced are important ways to make the business grow and prosper. Having the right location also has a lot to do with the ability to grow and profit.

"Picking the right location can be tricky, depending on the market," Patrick said. "If you're going after dealers, a storefront location may not be necessary. But if you want retail trade and repeat customers, good visibility and easy access are key."

You also need good employees to run a detailing shop, but finding them can be challenging, even though no special education is necessary to be a skillful detailing technician. Patrick suggested posting an ad in the local paper to drum up candidates. He also recognizes that because some of the best candidates actually come from the competition, it is important to offer whatever benefits you can to keep them.

"Employee retention usually is based on pay scale and the opportunity to grow within the company," he says. "Employees who show up regularly and on time, do good work, and have good people skills become very important to a small detailing business."

Patrick recommends tying your pricing strategy to the national averages for detailing. The national average for retail work today is about $200 for a full detail and about $100 for auto dealers. Of course, you can negotiate lower or higher prices depending on the level of service the customer desires or where you are doing business. In addition, he says you should price the job based on the vehicle's size and condition, as larger and dirtier vehicles take longer to detail and should cost more.

"Just consider that, depending on the condition of the vehicle, there can be roughly 10 to 20 different types of products for cleaning, dressing, and protection in a typical detailing," he said. "Then you need to use various tools, from an industrial buffer to extractors, vacuums, air compressor, fogger, and ozone machine. The more products you must use and the more time it takes to complete a job should be reflected in the price."

Despite his current success, Patrick admitted he could have done some things in the beginning to make the business go more smoothly.

"Knowing what I know now, I would have gotten more financial backing, which would have made the business grow faster," he says. "I started this business with $1,000 and slowly turned it into a worldwide, million-dollar business. I advise all would-be detailers to be an apprentice with another detailer or go through a professional training program such as what we offer at Appearance Plus. That's the best way to learn the tricks of the trade and learn how to market the business successfully."

# Defining Your Mission

There is one more piece of housekeeping to attend to before leaving this chapter: You should seriously consider writing a mission statement for your business.

A mission statement differs from a vision statement in that it defines the actual purpose of the business rather than that blue-sky version of what you hope to become. Big businesses have been crafting carefully worded mission statements for decades. They do it to define the scope of their business and have a benchmark against which to measure progress toward their goals.

Those are good reasons for you to write a mission statement, too. It will help to focus your thinking on the purpose and direction of your business, as well as your responsibilities to customers and services — and all of this wisdom will be encapsulated in just one or two paragraphs. On the other hand, you could emulate the example of PepsiCo Inc., which for years had what is arguably the most famous and succinct mission statement in history: "Beat Coke."

The point is: Your mission statement does not have to be lengthy, complicated, or convoluted. For example, here is a simple mission statement for a mobile detailer who specializes in big rigs: "CKL Mobile will offer quality detailing services of all kinds at the truck terminals located within a 40-mile radius of the Port of Long Beach."

Here is a longer mission statement that focuses on specialties:

> "To provide the best possible service to families and gear heads alike in the Minneapolis-St. Paul area, with a focus on basic services. Specialties will include the maintenance services necessary for a vehicle to survive a harsh Minnesota winter, as well as the cosmetic services that make cars shine and make their owners proud the rest of the year."

Finally, here is a mission statement that focuses on growth:

"Washing and waxing all makes and models of vehicles will be the purpose of Lou's Details, a one-person detailing business catering to business professionals that offers free pick-up and delivery service. Initially, Lou's will detail two cars a day, but by the end of the calendar year, and with the addition of one part-time employee, the business will handle three to four cars a day. This growth will occur by distributing leave-behind materials at the various office buildings and complexes in Lou's market area."

A mission statement can be as simple or as detailed as you wish, and you do not have to hire a marketing company to draft it. Rather, to come up with some ideas, use what is known as the "Five Ws (and One H)" approach — that is, who, what, where, when, why, and how statements — to focus your thinking.

Referring back to Lou's Details' mission statement, here is how to apply the method:

- **Who:** Lou's Details (technically, the "who" is Lou, because the business itself is inanimate, but this works, too)
- **What:** Detailing business professionals' cars
- **Where:** Office buildings and office complexes in Lou's market area
- **When:** Every business day
- **Why:** *(See below)*
- **How:** Working alone at first, then by adding one part-time employee

Notice that "why" is left blank. You could write a statement such as "To make money" or "To become the king of detailers and rule the Carnauba Empire." But neither of these is very useful, even though the desire to make money is at the heart of your motivation to start a detailing business. At the same time, a more professional statement such as "To build a viable business that will support my family" is certainly acceptable, but consider whether that information really figures into your business development and planning. In this case, it really does not. So it is all right to leave a W or the H blank if you cannot tie it to a professional business goal. Your next step is to take the answers you come up with in response to your "Five Ws (And One H)" questions, consider them, and draft a mission statement.

But now you are probably wondering exactly what you should do with your mission statement once you have it. You could post it above the cash register in your shop. You could reproduce it on your Web site. Or you could include it in your leave-behind service brochure. A lot of business owners, including detailers, do these things all the time. But a mission statement really only has value to the business owner. So frame it and hang it over the desk in your office instead. Just remember to look at it often; it is a good way to measure how your business is doing and to remind yourself what should be done every day.

# Chapter 4

## Legal and Administrative Details

Now that you have a good idea of exactly what a car detailer does and who will be revved up to use your services, it is time to start laying the foundation for your new business. While it is possible to kick off a detailing business with nothing more than a bucket of soapy water and a sponge, it is not a very professional way to do business. So in this chapter, you will find information concerning the process of selecting the right legal structure, picking an appropriate business name, and finding business professionals who can help steer your fledgling operation in the right direction.

## Making It Legal

One of the first tasks you must undertake as a new business owner is to choose a legal structure for your business. It is important to select wisely because this decision will impact everything related to your business, from your personal liability to the amount of taxes you will pay.

The four legal forms of ownership are the sole proprietorship, general partnership, corporation, and limited liability copmany (LLC). Many small-business owners, including detailers, tend to launch their businesses as sole proprietorships simply because it is the easiest legal entity to form. But simplicity is not always the best reason to go that route. Depending on your tax situation, you may find that another form would be more advantageous and would protect your business and personal assets better. For this reason, you should consult with an attorney who specializes in commercial law or an accountant who understands small-business matters. You will find more information on how to select these important business professionals later in this chapter. In the meantime, here is a look at each of the four legal structures and what kind of protection they offer.

## Sole proprietorship

From a paperwork standpoint, the sole proprietorship is the easiest and least expensive type of business to form. All you have to do is to start washing and waxing cars and, at tax time, file an extra form — IRS Schedule C (Form 1040): Profit or Loss From Business — and pay self-employment taxes. Depending on your state and local ordinances, you also may need a business license. But that is basically it. You own and manage the business, you own all its assets, and you reap all the profits. You also are personally responsible for all the business's debts and liabilities, which could include legal claims. That means both your personal and business assets are fair game in a lawsuit. Now, before you dismiss the possibility of a future lawsuit, consider this: You will be working with water, which opens up the possibility of a slip-and-fall accident. You could have a car owner go ballistic because you used the wrong wax on his or her Lamborghini, or you might be unable to fully repair a burn-through problem caused by a new turbo buffer. The main point to remember is that lawsuits can happen, even if you are operating a small sole proprietorship car detailing business.

When you are mulling over forming a sole proprietorship, consider your personal tolerance for risk. If you feel comfortable assuming risk and protecting yourself with business insurance rather than a legal decree, a sole proprietorship might be for you. If not, consider one of the other legal forms. Finally, if you plan to raise money to fund your business, a sole proprietorship definitely is not a viable option. Most banks or investors will not even speak to you if the business is not incorporated. The same thing goes for obtaining credit from vendors and suppliers. In particular, if your personal credit history is not stellar, suppliers may be reluctant to extend credit for the products you need to run the business.

## Partnership

Under a partnership, two or more people share the ownership and assets — as well as the debts and liabilities — of the business. Just like a sole proprietor, the partners report their income or loss from the business on their personal tax returns, and the partnership does not pay business taxes.

There are two types of partnerships. A general partnership is an arrangement between two or more people who are equal partners. This is the type of partnership most small-business owners choose. It is an especially good arrangement for people who have complementary skills. For example, you might be the detailing master, while your partner rocks the business-management side. On the other hand, you might find that a limited partnership suits your needs better. This is an arrangement between partners who do not share equal standing in the business. In this case, you might be the general partner who holds the controlling interest, with one or more limited partners whose contributions to the business are strictly financial. Limited partners have no involvement in decision-making for the business, and their profit is proportionate to the amount of their investment.

A partnership can be advantageous because you share insight, knowledge, and liability. But forming a business with another person is always risky, even if you know the person well. For that reason, you should have an attorney draw up articles of partnership before you launch the business. That way, if the partnership does not work out for some reason, or one partner dies or wishes to leave, then you have a clear plan for how the business will be divided, passed to heirs, or dissolved.

For more specifics about partnerships, check out IRS Publication 541, *Partnerships*, which is available at your local IRS office or online at **www.irs.gov.**

## Corporation

The chief advantage of a corporation is that it treats the business as a legal entity that is separate from its owner. This, in turn, limits the owner's personal liability when it comes to business debts, lawsuits, and judgments. So if you have a low tolerance for risk, a corporation makes a lot of sense. There is another good reason to form a corporation. As mentioned earlier, you may find that some companies, such as banks and suppliers, will do business with you only if you are incorporated. Even companies that contract out detailing services, such as auto dealerships, may be reluctant to turn over their shiny, new vehicles if you are not incorporated.

There are two types of corporations. The C corporation is considered to be the standard type of corporation. It offers the owner and his or her stockholders benefits, such as limited personal liability, as well as the ability to deduct ordinary business expenses and provide tax-free employee benefits, such as health and life insurance. But here is the catch: The profits of C corporations are subject to double taxation. A corporation pays federal and state taxes on its profits, then its employees and shareholders pay personal taxes on any money the corporation distributes.

The second type of corporation is the S corporation, and its chief benefit for small-business owners is that the company is not required to pay federal income taxes. Instead, like with a sole proprietorship or partnership, business profits are reported as ordinary income on the owners' personal income taxes (known as pass-through taxes). This does preserve more of the profits of the corporation, but an S corporation has more regulations and restrictions to contend with. For example, all owners of the S corporation must be U.S. citizens or resident aliens.

State governments require both types of corporations to file articles of incorporation, elect company officers and/or a board of directors, and hold an annual meeting. These meetings do not have to be formal; just make sure someone takes minutes and files a copy with your business records. You are probably aware that you can set up your own corporation using an online service. But because corporate law tends to be complicated, it is usually better to leave the task in the capable hands of an attorney instead.

## Limited liability company (LLC)

LLCs are popular with small-business owners such as detailers because they combine the tax advantages of a sole proprietorship or partnership, including pass-through taxation, while offering the limited liability of a corporation. Another benefit is that the management of an LLC is much more informal than that of a corporation because there are fewer paperwork requirements and there is no need for annual meetings. LLCs do have some disadvantages, the chief one being that the members of an LLC are subject to self-employment tax. In addition, some states tax LLCs, even though they do not tax corporations. Because state laws govern LLCs, consult with your attorney or tax adviser about whether an LLC is an appropriate choice for you.

# Naming Rights — and Wrongs

New business owners usually enjoy the task of choosing a business name. It is fun to brainstorm, come up with crazy and catchy names, and debate the merits of each one before settling on the perfect moniker. But a little restraint is in order here. You want your business name to be unique, but at the same time, it needs to sound professional and evocative of what you do. Take a look at these names of detailing shops around the country:

- All Washed Up
- Bling Mobile Pressure Wash and Detail

- Classic Appreciation
- Dr. Dent & Detailing
- Dynamic Detailing
- KLS Custom Detailing
- Mad Doctor Mobile Car Wash
- Madrigal's Elite Mobile Detailing
- Mr. Detail Auto Salon
- T-Bones
- The Original Absolute

Although you were probably drawn to the clever or fun names, they are not necessarily the best ones on the list. For example, All Washed Up could belong to a coin-laundry service or a self-serve car wash. Likewise, T-Bones sounds more like a collision shop, as in the place where "T-boned" vehicles are stashed until the insurance company writes them off. In addition, some of the names do not evoke detailing, such as Classic Appreciation or The Original Absolute.

The intent here is not to criticize detailers who are successfully doing business under these names. Creativity can be a good thing, especially because a clever name could make a business more memorable in a large field of competitors. But the point is, when you are trying to build visibility for a business, you do not want to choose a name that is too obscure. There is a way to have your clever name and business recognition, too. Just add something about the type of business operation after the name. For example, if you add "auto detailing" after T-Bones or The Original Absolute, the function becomes crystal clear. The same goes for names such as Rick's Auto Detailing Café or Capt'n Jack's Detailing Cove. Have fun with the name if you wish, but be practical, too.

## Claim your name

Incidentally, all the names listed above are known as trade names. A trade name is the official name of the business and is used on the company's bank accounts, letterhead, and other official documents. It is more commonly known as an assumed name or a "DBA," short for "doing business as," and it may or may not be trademarked.

Although most businesses must register their trade name as a way of identifying who owns the business, there is one exception. A sole proprietor who uses his or her full, legal name as part of the business name is not required to file for a DBA. For example, John J. Lambert Auto Detailing contains the full legal name of its sole proprietor owner, so it does not need to be registered, whereas Lambert Auto Detailing is a trade name that must be registered officially.

Local governments — usually at the county level — issue a DBA to a company. Registration gives you exclusive use of the name, but only in the jurisdiction where you filed for it. If you plan to do business in more than one jurisdiction, as would be the case for a mobile detailer or franchise owner, you would need to file multiple DBA forms. You also may be required to publish a fictitious name/DBA statement in a general circulation newspaper for a certain length of time — often four weeks. The agency issuing your DBA can tell you whether your state requires this. The cost for a DBA registration is quite nominal, usually between $10 and $60, depending on where you are doing business. You can use the name for five years and simply renew it when it expires. After applying for a DBA, the county will conduct a search to make sure your name is unique before you are granted permission to use it, so have a few names in mind just in case your first choice is not available.

You can do your own DBA search to get an idea of which names are already in use, both by detailers and other businesses. Start by checking the detailing-company listings in your phone book. Next, try doing a trademark search on the U.S. Patent and Trademark Office Web site at **www.uspto.gov**. Finally, look on search engines for the name. You might be shocked to see how many companies, even non-detailers, already use your dream name, which means you will have to come up with another one.

Speaking of trademarks, it is important to note that while DBA will give you the use of the name in your local area, it is not the same thing as a trademark. The latter is a distinctive word, phrase, symbol, or other device that uniquely identifies and distinguishes your products and/or services from others in the marketplace. If your detailing business takes off and you decide to trademark the name at a later date, you will have to register the trademark with the U.S. Patent and Trademark Office, and you may find the name has already been taken. So if you really want to protect your company name, you might consider applying for a trademark right away. It is important to mention branding, which refers to the symbol or name that identifies your business and separates it from your competition. In some cases, a logo can be copyrighted, too. Go to the USPTO Web site for more information. This should not be confused with your trade name, which is the name under which you are doing business. Here is an example: NBC is the brand name for the National Broadcasting Co. Its highly recognizable peacock logo is part of NBC's overall branding strategy.

As you embark on your new detailing venture, you probably will not be thinking about anything beyond finding customers and making money. But branding builds recognition and loyalty among customers. It also reinforces your company's message of quality and reliability and, as such, should be on your mind early in the business-development process.

Therefore, draft a logo and use it on everything related to the business, from your printed materials and Web site to your exterior sign if you own a brick-and-mortar facility. Then, deliver on the promise of that brand by providing the best detailing service and customer service. Through word of mouth and your own promotional and marketing activities, your brand recognition will grow and, ultimately, you can become a leader in auto detailing in your market area.

# Other Operational Issues

There are a few other operational ducks you must get in a row before you can embark on your new detailing business. They include:

1. **Applying for an employer identification number (EIN):** All business owners (except sole proprietors) are required to have this federal ID number, which is used when you file your business tax return. Sole proprietors continue to use their Social Security numbers. You can apply for an EIN online at **www.irs.gov** or by calling 1-800-829-4933.

2. **Complying with OSHA regulations:** The Occupational Safety and Health Administration oversees everything re-

lated to workplace safety and worker injuries and illnesses. For instance, it requires businesses that use hazardous chemicals to maintain a file of Material Safety Data Sheets (MSDS), which provide information about the chemical's properties and potential health hazards. Because OSHA has only about 1,100 inspectors, the chances of your having an unannounced workplace inspection are pretty low. But if a complaint is ever lodged against your shop, an inspector will drop in at some point, and the penalty for proven workplace violations is steep. For that reason, it is a good idea to get OSHA safety and health training. Contact your local OSHA office or visit **www.osha.gov** for more information. The good news: If you are a sole proprietor or you have no employees, you are exempt from OSHA oversight, but it is good to practice workplace safety nonetheless.

3. **Understanding employment law:** Any business that has employees must comply with Title VI of the Civil Rights Act of 1964, which prevents discrimination on the basis of race, color, or national origin. Employers also must have each new hire fill out Form I-9, which verifies eligibility to work in the U.S. In addition, you must know about the Fair Labor Standards Act, which governs workplace wages and hours, and workers' compensation, the state-mandated insurance that covers employees who are injured on the job. Finally, some states (like California) have a registration and employment law that applies to car washes and detailers. Your attorney can help you understand all these issues to make sure you stay on the right side of the law.

4. **Observing water usage and hazardous waste disposal requirements:** Auto detailing requires water, and wastewater must be reclaimed or treated rather than just being discharged into sewer systems. Your state's department of environmental quality may have additional regulations concerning the disposal of chemicals and paints used for detailing. Check with your local government to find out what the requirements are.

5. **Obtaining a business license:** Most municipalities require businesses within their borders to be licensed. At the local level, this is more a formality than anything, and the cost of the license is usually quite nominal. To apply for a license, you will need your EIN and DBA paperwork, as well as a checking account set up in the business's name. Licenses are renewable annually, and you usually have to appear in person to apply. Your state may have specific licensing requirements, as well. In Michigan, for example, the state requires auto detailers to be certified in order to do business. Contact your state's division of licensing to find out what is necessary.

6. **Applying for permits:** Among the types of permits a detailer may need are a building permit if you are remodeling an existing structure; a zoning compliance permit, which verifies that your commercial space is zoned properly for the business; and a seller's permit, which you will need to purchase merchandise such as detailing supplies for resale to customers. You also will need a state sales-tax license when selling retail products.

That is a lot of paperwork to fill out and procedures to adhere to. If you need help sorting through the red tape, consult with an attorney or go straight to your local and state governments for guidance.

# Hiring Business Advisers

At the dawn of your new business, the last thing you might be thinking about is bringing people on board to share the work. In fact, unless you are launching a site-based business, it is usually advisable *not* to hire anyone right away because the early years of a new business tend to be pretty lean, financially speaking. That said, there are several different business professionals you should consider using on a contract or hourly basis to assist with necessary administrative tasks. They include an attorney, an accountant, an insurance broker, and a computer consultant. If you are planning to open a stand-alone detailing shop, you should add a space planner to that list as well.

There are two very good reasons to farm out some of your administrative work. First, you are going into business to be a detailer, not a bookkeeper, computer troubleshooter, or law expert. Second, you are probably *not* as well versed in those disciplines as professionals. So it makes more sense to do the work you like, which is detailing, rather than trying to handle the stuff you are not as experienced or skilled in. Here is a look at each of the business professionals you should consider adding to your management team.

**Attorney:** Some people are intimidated by the idea of even occupying the same space as an attorney, probably because of all those clever TV lawyer shows such as *Boston Legal*. But as a new business owner, it is important for you to establish a relationship with an attorney now, before you actually need one. As mentioned earlier, an attorney can help you select the most advantageous legal structure for your business.

He or she also can be a resource for reviewing contracts, whether you are contracting for products or services or signing a lease on a building. Finally, an attorney is your advocate if legal disputes or lawsuits arise. To find an attorney, ask business acquaintances or your banker for recommendations. You also can visit Web sites such as **www.findanattorney.com** or **www.lawyers.com** for leads. Although many lawyers work on retainer, you usually can contract for services on a project or hourly basis, which helps keep the cost down.

**Accountant:** There is a lot at stake when you start a new business, and making a mistake on the corporate taxes or financial records is not an option. Enter your local, friendly accountant or bookkeeper, who can keep those financial details straight by setting up recordkeeping systems, taking charge of your income-tax filings so they are submitted on time, interpreting tax law, keeping track of your income and expenses, and making your small business run as smoothly as possible. Self-employed accountants are usually the best choice for a small-business owner because their hourly rates are lower. As when searching for an attorney, ask business acquaintances for leads to an accountant.

Although you should have an accountant, you should not turn over management of the finances completely and never look at the books yourself. A software program such as Intuit® QuickBooks is easy to use and helps you track income and expenses, create invoices, and perform other useful financial tasks that every business owner should at least have a nodding acquaintance with.

**Insurance broker:** Strictly speaking, an insurance broker is not part of your business team like an attorney or accountant is, because you will need his or her services less often. But you still need someone to call regarding insurance coverage or questions about your policies. Detailers actually require a lot of insurance to operate, all of which is discussed later in this chapter, and it can be difficult and time-consuming to run down all those policies on your own. An insurance broker does not work for any one particular insurer and therefore can search for suitable policies and favorable rates among all the companies.

**Computer consultant:** Even if you enjoy tinkering with computers and unraveling electronic conundrums, you probably will not have enough time in the day to be both a computer technician and a car detailer. So find a consultant who makes house calls and can take care of everything from hardware and software installation to optimizing your hard drive and killing viruses.

**Space planner:** You will need this professional only if you decide to open a site-based facility. Unless you happen to stumble upon a detailing shop or even a service station for sale that meets your needs, you will need help from a facility specialist to set up an efficient workspace. *The various areas needed in a detailing shop are discussed at length in Chapter 6.* But if you would like to see what a typical detailing-shop work area looks like, check out RL "Bud" Abraham's Web site, **www.detailplus.com**, where you can find sample layouts. Abraham also sells shop layout plans and consulting services to help you put together an efficient shop. If you have the knack, you can use software packages to design your own space. One you can try is SmartDraw, which offers a free trial demo at **www.smartdraw.com**.

# Protecting Your Assets

As mentioned earlier, car detailers have some extensive insurance needs, especially if they have employees and a work facility. The primary type of insurance you need is commercial garage keeper's liability insurance. It covers clients' vehicles when they are in your care and also protects them against damage caused by fire, theft, or collision. Detailing-industry experts recommend purchasing $1 million to $2 million of coverage, even if you own a one-person mobile shop. That might sound like a lot, but it is a standard policy amount in this industry.

If you own or lease a building, property insurance is a must. Also known as casualty insurance, this type of policy protects the building and everything in it in case of fire, vandalism, and weather-related damage. The policy's cost is based on the property's value and contents.

Workers' compensation insurance is required in every state, although in Texas, it is possible for private employers to opt out of the workers' comp system. This "no-fault" insurance protects employees who sustain work-related injuries, as well as those whose illnesses or diseases can be traced to the workplace. Because detailers use a lot of chemicals in their line of work, the idea of work-related illness is not as far-fetched as it might seem. Only a company's employees are covered by workers' comp. As the employer, you do not qualify for workers' comp benefits if you are injured or incapacitated. The issue of workers' comp is too complex to discuss fully here, so ask your attorney for guidance.

You might not be covered personally under workers' compensation, but you have a lot to lose if you have to shut down your business because of a natural disaster, fire, or other unavoidable loss. So, you may want to consider business interruption insurance, which can cover your normal business expenses until your company is up and running again. Because you will have flammable liquids on board your mobile unit or in your shop, the cost of business interruption insurance may end up being a little high. But when you weigh it against the cost of losing everything and going out of business, the cost of this insurance seems less onerous.

Other types of insurance that can be beneficial for a detailer include bonding, which is protection against loss caused by employees who steal from the business or its clients; disability, which replaces a percentage of your gross income if you are unable to work; health insurance, which you will need to fund yourself as a self-employed person and is 100 percent deductible as a business expense; and life insurance, which protects your family in the event of your death. A financial institution also may require life insurance when you apply for financing.

And there you have it: everything and everyone you need to protect your business and give it the best chance of success. In the next chapter, you will learn about what is arguably the most important document you will need to run your business: a detailed business plan. This, more than anything, is the real key to success.

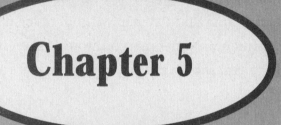

# Chapter 5

## Mapping Out the Business

In the course of life, everyone collects a lot of important documents: a passport, a marriage license, mortgage papers, and birth certificates. Now that you are an entrepreneur, you will add another important document to your collection: a business plan.

A business plan is like a road map: At any given moment in your business's evolution, it tells you where you are and where you are headed. It helps you think proactively, as well as recognize what you have done that has benefited the business and what you should never do again. Incredibly, a lot of small-business owners never take the time to write a formal business plan. Sometimes it is because they do not need to borrow start-up money and so were not forced to put their ideas and master plan on paper for the bank. Sometimes they get so caught up in the process of trying to make money that everything else falls to the wayside. And sometimes they simply think it is not important. But none of these is a good reason to skip this important step in the development of your business. The reason you need a business plan is simple:

Without a plan, you are not in control of your own destiny. You would not set out on a cross-country trip without maps from the auto club or a folder full of Internet map printouts. Likewise, you should not attempt to embark on the journey to business success without a viable plan.

Although this chapter is devoted entirely to the process of creating a business plan, do not think you have to turn out a 100-page document or spend the next year of your life writing your plan instead of detailing cars. In fact, if the purpose of your plan is to keep your business on track rather than to seek financing, you can jot your ideas down as a simple bulleted list rather than writing a massive document with all the bells and whistles.

The entire gamut of the business plan experience is discussed here just in case you do need a more formalized plan to seek financing — or if you are determined to do up this business the right way from the start.

# The Components of a Business Plan

Although you can write a business plan that discusses both the grand scheme and the minutiae of a company's operation, it is not necessary to go into that kind of detail for a detailing business, especially if you are establishing a one-person business. In that case, simply considering the big picture as it pertains to your first year of operation will suffice to get your business off the ground. If you will have a bigger operation and need employees to run it, a more detailed business plan is a good idea. No matter which way you go, here are the basic components of a business plan and what they should cover:

1. **Cover sheet:** This is an easy task to kick off the business-plan writing process. Your cover sheet should give the name of your company, the legal form of operation — *refer to Chapter 4 for discussion of each* — and contact information for the primary contact person, who likely will be you.

2. **Executive summary:** This section summarizes the entire plan, usually in a few hundred words. You will mention your business model (specifically, your business concept and purpose), a list of the services you will offer, the business's legal form of operation, and your overall goals. The purpose of an executive summary is to give a glimpse of what the business plan contains without having to read the entire document. It also should be the last thing you write because it is an overview of the entire plan. The easiest way to write it is to look through the body of the plan for ideas and rewrite them for the executive summary.

3. **Description of the business:** Here you will outline the scope of your services and your responsibilities, both for your own edification and for that of any future investors or financiers. When discussing your services, you need to say more than just, "I detail cars." Rather, discuss each service you will offer, from your full detail service to any special services you have on tap, and provide some details about what they entail. *Feel free to use any part or the entire "Detailing Basics" list in Chapter 2 for this part of your plan.* You also will want to outline your business objectives

here. Now, your main objective is no doubt to make money to support you and your family. But all that goes without saying. Focus instead on writing goals that are S.M.A.R.T. — specific, measurable, attainable, realistic, and trackable. This is a technique used in both project and performance management that can help you arrive at objectives to help move your business forward. To make your goals specific (often a tricky task), attack the process using the "Five Ws (and One H)" process. *See this method outlined in Chapter 3.* Here is an example: Your general goal might be to "get new business." The specific goal could be "join the chamber of commerce (*what*) to meet other business people (*who*) and exchange business cards (*how*)."

4. **Market strategies:** In Chapter 3, you learned how to analyze your market area and identify your target audience. Now, you will use the information to figure out how to make that audience aware of your services. Toward that end, you need to create an integrated approach to marketing, using everything from advertising and word of mouth to promotional materials and a Web site. The goal is to make your market aware of your brand, increase your credibility as a capable business provider, and increase awareness of your services every way you can. Mull that over and list these tactics in this section of your business plan.

5. **Competitive analysis:** This is one of the most crucial parts of your business plan. You need to identify both your direct and indirect competition to figure out a plan for standing out among them. *As a starting point, refer to the list of possible competitors in Chapter 1.* Then give some thought

to whom you believe you are competing against in your market, from the detailer across town to the car wash next door. Do an Internet search to help with the process. List these companies by name. Next, consider what you can do to make your business unique. Maybe it is offering free pick-up and delivery, when the other detailers charge for the same service. Or maybe you could offer free trunk shampooing, when the others offer only vacuuming. Implement ideas such as these to bring in new business, and detail those ideas in this section.

6. **Operational and management plan:** Write a description of the day-to-day operations of your business for this part of the plan. *You can use the information in Chapter 2 as a blueprint.* Talk about the experience and background of the principals of the business, starting with yourself as owner. Information about operating expenses goes in this section as well. *In Chapter 12, you will learn how to create an income and expense statement that will provide the type of information you will need here.*

7. **Financial data:** This should include documents such as an income statement, a balance sheet, and a 12-month cash-flow analysis. A break-even analysis is also a must, as it shows exactly how many services you will need to perform to meet your operating obligations and start making a profit. You can use a software program such as Business Plan Pro ($99.95 from **www.paloalto.com**) to draft these documents, or you can have your accountant do the deed. Then, summarize the information in your spreadsheets in

your business plan. Attach copies of the spreadsheets in an appendix to the report.

8. **Additional information:** Other sections may have a place in your plan, such as a discussion of personnel and insurance coverage — in short, anything related to the business that will give someone who knows nothing about it a well-rounded view. In addition, include other relevant supporting documents in an appendix, such as a copy of your franchise agreement, if applicable; a copy of your building lease or deed; copies of pertinent legal documents, including the partnership agreement or DBA papers; and copies of the management team's résumés.

As someone who spiffs up vehicles for a living, you are sure to appreciate the need to make your completed business plan look as neat and professional as possible. Print it on white or cream 8.5- by 11-inch paper. Make sure it is free of errors, because nothing says "amateur" more than a document riddled with spelling and grammatical errors. Have an experienced editor or proofreader give the document the once-over, checking for logical development and completeness, as well as those pesky spelling and grammar mistakes.

Next, even if you are the only one who will see it, put your business plan in a binder or a sturdy folder, both of which are available at a local office superstore. That gives it the importance it deserves as your master plan for success. Place it in a prominent spot right on top of your desk where you can see it every day. Never stash it in a bottom drawer where you will forget about it. You absolutely must refer to your business plan frequently, both to verify that your plans are on track and to make necessary course corrections to keep them there. You also need to update the plan periodically to set new goals and respond to developing market conditions.

# Free Help, No Waiting

If you are feeling daunted by the prospect of writing a business plan because writing is not your strong suit, never fear. A couple of excellent resources are available to you at no cost. The first is SCORE Association, a national, nonprofit organization of working and retired executives who provide free counseling and advice to aspiring business owners in all fields. In addition to on-site mentoring, the organization offers educational workshops on topics such as business-plan development, pricing, marketing, managing finances, and more. To find one of the 370 SCORE offices near you, go to **www.score.org** and plug in your ZIP code. If the nearest office is too far away for easy access, feel free to call, or ask a question on the online mentoring form. Also be sure to look at the testimonials under the "Success Stories" link to get inspired about how SCORE can help you.

The second useful resource is the Small Business Administration (SBA) at **www.sba.gov**. Click on "Small Business Planner" to find useful tools, including information about crafting a business plan. The site also has a link to sample business plans for various types of businesses, including an automobile restoration business that, although not an exact match for a detailing business, can give you some ideas on what to include and how to format your own plan. You also might want to complete the online "How to Prepare a Business Plan" tutorial to get some hands-on experience. *Also see the sample business plan for a detailing business in Appendix A of this book.* It may be much longer than what you eventually produce, but it is a good starting point and will give you an idea of how to format the various sections.

## CASE STUDY: OVERCOMING OBSTACLES

Todd and Anthony Tabacco
Q-Tipp Treatment
1003 Route 22
Brewster, N.Y. 10509
Phone: 845-278-0038

Todd and Anthony Tabacco have owned Q-Tipp Treatment for the past 12 years. Todd has made full use of his bachelor's degree in business management in the running of the business, while brother Anthony has taken advantage of his bachelor's degree in marketing to help make the business the success it is today. With one shop in Brewster, New York, clientele at Q-Tipp Treatment range from lawyers and doctors to construction workers and housewives.

"We had a little trouble [attracting customers] at first because detailing was not as well-known then as it is today," Todd said. "We had to explain the difference between our services and those of a local car wash. We overcame [the obstacles] simply by showing customers the equipment we use and examples of cars with completed detailing jobs."

The company specializes in paintless dent removal, carpet dyeing, and complete and express detailing. The brothers work with both car dealerships and individuals. The company also runs the new-car departments for a couple of dealerships. At one time, they tinted windows and did pinstriping, but they dropped these services to focus more on detailing.

"I chose this business because it was always something we did growing up," Todd explained. "We would help my father wash, clean, and wax his vehicles. When I finished college, I was disappointed by the job choices available and decided to go into business for myself. My brother felt the same way, so we became partners."

Todd does admit it was hard to get steady work at first. "I landed a dealer account, which made me busy," he said. "Then we needed more help, so hiring became the next obstacle to overcome. Next, we needed more equipment, so we took a small loan from our father so we could buy the equipment needed to keep up with the volume of business. And yes, we did pay him back."

Todd says Q-Tipp Treatment did very little advertising in the beginning, yet still managed to land business. They used the PennySaver and the Yellow Pages to spread the word about who they were and what they were doing. But he admits that even now, the best advertising is always word of mouth driven by satisfied customers. Todd credits his partnership with his brother for the overall success of Q-Tipp Treatment. While they often see things in different ways, they are able to talk and negotiate when differences arise — a process that also helps generate fresh and innovative ideas.

"This business is successful because of the hard work we put in," he added. "At first, that meant working seven days a week, but as the business grew, we were able to cut back a little. However, we still work a lot. The other thing that has made us successful is our workers. They are a product of what Q-Tipp has become. And seven years ago, our father retired, and he has been working with us part-time ever since."

Despite the success of the business, Todd said he could have done things a little differently in the formative years. For instance, he would have installed a Detail Plus system earlier.

"It makes us run more efficiently because everything is at our fingertips," he said. "If we had to go back to the old way, we would give up detailing."

In addition to an efficient system, Todd said that patience is necessary to be really successful.

"Rome wasn't built in a day, after all," he says. "It's natural to want to grow every year, but you don't want to grow too fast because your quality will go down. Also, it takes great sacrifice and commitment to be successful. You may not take home a check at first. However, if you reinvest in your business, you will be a success."

Todd feels that, in the future, the location of a detailing shop will continue to be important, perhaps even more so than it is now. He recommends locating a new business near auto dealerships because they are a good source of potential customers. In addition, the dealerships probably already have investigated the local demographics to see if the area can support the volume of business they need to stay successful. You should be able to trust their judgment, he says, which means you probably can avoid doing extensive market research as part of your marketing planning. Finally, dealerships attract lookers, and you may be able to attract some of those customers as well.

The Tabacco brothers appreciate their employees, but they still work hard to find and retain good people. For the most part, Todd uses publications such as the PennySaver to attract new help, but he also tends to ask his current employees if they know anyone looking for a job.

"Current employees probably wouldn't recommend anyone bad because it could affect their own reputation with the company," Todd said. "We constantly interview people and keep them on file even if we are not hiring. We do this so when we do need help, we don't have to choose whoever comes through the door."

The Tabaccos do their best to be bosses their employees can relate to and respect, since this is the best way to motivate them and keep them happy.

"You have to try to be equal and fair," Todd emphasized. "However, you still have to be strict and direct in order to gain an employee's respect. When I hire a new employee, the main qualities I look for are a good attitude, good work ethic, and referrals, among other things."

While pricing is certainly an important part of the success equation, Todd noted that they charge their dealers less because of the volume of work they throw their way. When quoting on work for other customers, he bases prices on factors such as the size of the vehicle, its overall condition, and whether it is used commercially. Other factors such as whether there is a lot of animal hair to clean up, a lot of scratches both inside and out, or significant overspray will impact the pricing.

Depending on the vehicle, Q-Tipp Treatment technicians may use as many as ten to 15 chemicals in the course of detailing. Although they use standard equipment such as carpet extractors, vacuums, orbital and high-speed buffers, compressors, and pressure washers, the Tabaccos feel they have an advantage with the Detail Plus system, which puts products right at hand where they are needed. But one of the most rewarding parts of the job at Q-Tipp Treatment is turning over the finished product to the customer.

"I love when you can make a bad car look good," Todd said. "It does not matter if it is the stains on the inside that have been taken out or the scratches on the outside that make the car look better. Whatever makes the customer go 'Wow' is what I like best."

Chapter 6

Setting Up Shop

I t is probably safe to assume that one of the reasons you are
interested in starting a car detailing business is because the actual work might not seem like work: Revving up the orbital polisher or experimenting with new products can be a lot of fun for
a car buff. So, this chapter covers the various detailing tools and
products you will need to wash and shine customers' vehicles
to gleaming perfection. It also discusses the office tools you will
need to run your business as a professional enterprise.

# Your Detailing Needs

Before we get to the fun stuff, it bears mentioning that you should
always start a new detailing business using the tools and products you already have instead of dropping a lot of dough on shiny,
new equipment. Your mission here is to keep your start-up costs
as low as possible to have the best chance of success in the early
days. So avoid the temptation to roam up and down the aisles

of the local auto superstore and gleefully load up your basket, or the compulsion to surf the Internet for the latest and greatest gadgets. After all, it is possible to embark on a lucrative detailing career with just the bare necessities, and being in austerity mode when you start up definitely is good for your business's financial health. When the business begins turning a profit, you can upgrade your equipment.

On the other hand, if the equipment you have is in poor condition, balky, not powerful enough, or otherwise deficient, you *should* consider replacing it before you start detailing for a living. Having tools in good condition makes a positive impression on customers and increases their confidence that you can restore their rides to showroom condition. The tools and products discussed here are useful to site-based and mobile detailers alike. But mobile detailers do have unique needs because they have to carry everything along with them on every job. *You will find a section with tips for the mobile detailer later in this chapter.*

## Indispensable tools

Here is a list of the types of power equipment used in a detailing shop:

### Exterior washing/waxing

- **Pressure washer:** Used for general washing and engine detailing/degreasing. Kärcher® pressure systems is a well-known brand.

- **High-speed buffer:** Used for forceful paint correction and removal of imperfections such as scratches, swirls, and water spots. Most detailers have more than one in their arsenal at all times in case one goes kaput. Professional brands include the Dewalt® Heavy Duty Variable Speed buffer and the Makita® Variable Speed buffer.

- **Random orbital polisher:** Used for applying and removing wax and sealants, as well as for filling minor scratches with glazes or polish to minimize their appearance. Both the PPG Porter® Cable Dual Action Polisher and the Cyclo® Dual Head Polisher are good choices.

- **GEM orbital polisher:** Made by GEM Industries Inc., this polisher is a must for removing swirl marks left behind by high-speed buffers, as well as for applying wax and sealants.

#### Interior washing/odor removal

- **Air compressor:** Used for cleaning small spaces and powering pneumatic tools. Campbell Hausfeld and Hitachi are leading brands, while Tornador makes blowout and foam brush tools that attach to any model compressor.

- **Carpet extractor:** Used for cleaning carpeting, floor mats, and upholstery. Mytee Products Inc. and Detail Plus supply good brands of carpet extractors. Alternatively, you can use a rotary brush shampooer available from Detail Plus, which is especially effective for scrubbing carpet that is excessively soiled.

- **Wet/dry vacuum:** A less powerful alternative to a carpet extractor. As long as it has a 5 HP motor, a wet/dry vacuum should be adequate until you can invest in an extractor. You can pick up an affordable wet/dry vacuum at The Home Depot or department stores such as Target or Sears. Virtually any brand will do.

- **Ozone odor remover:** A powerful piece of equipment for removing odors and destroying bacteria, viruses, and mold. Detail King offers several commercial models you might want to check into at **www.detailking.com**.

- **Odor fogger system:** This electric thermal fogger discharges chemicals into a vehicle's interior to remove a wide variety of odors, from tobacco and pet odors to food and milk-spill odors. Top of the Line Detailing Supplies (**www. topoftheline.com**) sells a fogger system that should meet your needs.

- **Interior dryer:** Used for speeding up interior and exterior drying, even in the winter. Interior dryers are available at most detail supply companies.

You may be able to purchase turnkey detailing systems that include everything you need for a site-based operation. *You will find some leads to such systems in Appendix D.*

## Basic tools and supplies

In addition to the tools listed above, here is a comprehensive checklist of the types of detailing products you may need to do your job well:

### General tools and detailing supplies

- Stainless-steel tank sprayer (for everything except acid)

- Foam-pad cleaning tools
- Chamois polishing cloth
- Wash mitts
- Nylon bug sponge
- Terry-cloth or microfiber towels
- Towel wringer
- Spray and squeeze bottles
- Wire brush
- Nylon brushes
- Detail brushes
- Razor-blade scraper
- Single-edge razor blades
- Ultra-fine steel wool or sandpaper
- Sandpaper (2,000 grit)
- Heat gun
- Assorted polishing pads
- Finishing pads
- Wool-and-foam cutting pads
- Bonnets for your orbital
- Paint leveler
- Wax applicators
- Floor mats and seat covers
- Mechanic's creeper (for sliding under vehicles)

## Detailing products

- Car-wash soap (a.k.a. shampoo)
- Tar and grease remover
- Adhesive remover
- Extractor shampoo (non-foaming)
- Stain removers
- Carpet and vinyl dyes
- Carpet shampoo (foaming)

- All-purpose cleaner
- Fabric protectant
- Leather cleaner and conditioner
- Clay bars
- Water spot remover
- Rubbing compounds (heavy, medium, light, microfine)
- Degreaser
- Tire and wheel cleaners
- Acid-free wheel cleaner
- Glass polish
- Dressing for tire, engines, and interiors
- Carnauba wax
- Paint sealant
- Chrome polish

Detailing product brands abound. You are probably familiar with Meguiar's® products, which are popular among driveway detailers. They work great, but detailing professionals should use only professional-grade products, both to give the impression that you are a professional and because they come in economy-size containers at wholesale prices.

It is usually easiest to order detailing equipment, tools, and products online, although if you happen to work near a distribution center, you are likely to get personal service from a product representative who will bring merchandise right to your door. Otherwise, you can check out the wholesale Internet suppliers, some of which offer their own proprietary brands, and others that carry the professional products mentioned above and everything else a detailer needs.

# Details on Wheels

Mobile detailers certainly need most, if not all, of the same equipment and products as site-based detailers. But their challenge is transporting everything — from the smallest nylon brush to a tank of fresh water — to the job site and back in the most efficient and cost-effective way possible. The easiest and most professional way to do this is with a mobile-detailing trailer. You can buy everything from a trailer-mounted detailing system consisting of basic washing equipment and a power generator, to a more elaborate closed-trailer system that also has room to stock products and tools right inside. Both of these are designed to hook onto the back of a pick-up truck (preferably) or a van, which means you can use your vehicle during off hours sans trailer.

A detailing trailer starts at about $2,200 for the trailer alone to more than $10,000 for a fully outfitted, enclosed trailer. If you have the cash, go for the closed model because it has space for graphics on the outside, effectively turning it into a mobile billboard that promotes your business every time you take to the streets.

Alternately, if you need to start your business on the cheap and have a truck that you can sacrifice for the cause, you can purchase what is known as a skid-mount wash system that fits into the vehicle's bed. These systems typically come with a 100-gallon water tank, a generator and pump system, and a high-pressure hose. A standard truck toolbox or other lockbox is also a good idea so you can securely carry the other equipment and supplies you will need.

Because mobile detailers work in the great outdoors, it is always a good idea to consider buying a pop-up tent for those days when you are detailing outside, both to stay dry and to keep the sun off those delicate paint finishes. By the same token, a space heater you can power off the trailer generator for cool mornings and a shop light for late nights are other useful tools to invest in.

## Corralling the crud

One thing that has made mobile detailers somewhat less popular with some municipalities is their tendency to discharge dirty, soapy water into the local sewer system after they have spiffed and polished a vehicle. This is more than just a public relations snafu — some local governments hand out fines for this environmentally unfriendly habit. For this reason, stay on good terms with Mother Nature (and the Environmental Protection Agency) and tote a wastewater-reclamation system along with you. These systems consist of a car-wash mat, a vacuum system for sucking up wastewater so it stays out of the sewer system, and a holding tank for the recovered wastewater.

The following chart lists companies that offer detailing products, trailers, skid-mount systems, and water reclamation equipment.

| Company | Detailing Products (wholesale) | Detailing Trailers | Skid-mount Systems | Water Reclamation Equipment |
|---|---|---|---|---|
| Chemical Guys, www.chemicalguys.com | ✓ | | | |
| Detail King, www.detailking.com | ✓ | ✓ | ✓ | ✓ |
| Detail Plus Car Appearance Systems, www.detailplus.com | ✓ | ✓ | ✓ | |
| Details in Motion, www.detailtrailers.com | | ✓ | ✓ | |
| Detail Supply Outlet, www.detailsupplyoutlet.com | ✓ | ✓ | | |
| Eureka Lubricants, www.eurekalubricants.com | ✓ | | | |
| Kleen-Rite Corp., www.kleen-ritecorp.com | ✓ | | | |
| National Detail Systems, www.nationaldetail.com | | ✓ | ✓ | |
| Right Look, www.rightlook.com | | ✓ | | |
| Top of the Line, www.topoftheline.com | ✓ | | ✓ | ✓ |
| Ultimate Washer, www.ultimatewasher.com | | ✓ | | |
| Woods Pressure Washing, www.woodspressurewashers.com | | | | |

# Dressing for Success

No matter whether you will be a one-person enterprise or a detail-shop owner, you will want to look neat and professional while on the job. Adopting a uniform consisting of a wrinkle-free shirt or polo shirt and a hat — personalized with your company name — will do a lot to give you that professional image. But here is a heads-up: T-shirts are too casual, even if they are personalized, and in fact will make you look more like someone who just decided to make a few bucks that day washing cars than a legitimate business owner.

You do not have to buy a large number of shirts or hats when you order. Most companies will make up as few as one embroidered shirt or hat at a time, if that is all you need, at a reasonable price. In fact, one company picked at random on the Internet (**www.logosportswear.com**) charges $31 each for embroidered polo shirts with no minimum order and no set-up fees, and $22.95 each for embroidered baseball caps. At those prices, a one-person detailing business would spend less than $180, plus tax and shipping, to get five shirts, one cap, and the professional image he or she needs.

Two more items you should add to your work ensemble are protective hearing and eye gear. You will be working with power tools for long stretches of time, so preserve your hearing by always using earplugs or a hearing protector. In addition, all that sanding will throw off a lot of airborne particles, and detailing chemicals give off noxious fumes. A set of safety glasses can help keep particulate matter and irritating fumes out of your eyes. In fact, you might want to invest in some disposable masks to keep potentially harmful contaminants out of your lungs, too.

# Outfitting Your Office

While it may feel like your mobile detailing rig is your office, everyone — including both mobile and detailing-shop owners

— needs to have an office to pay bills, balance the books, and otherwise act like a small-business owner.

Unless you are planning to open a detailing shop and can eke out some office space there, the nerve center of your detailing empire is likely to be based in your home. Working from a home office is not only convenient, but it is also cost-effective because you can write off the portion of your home that you use for business on IRS Schedule C (Form 1040). So, find a nook or cranny in your home that you can dedicate to your business, such as a repurposed walk-in closet with folding doors or the bonus space above your garage, or — better still — commandeer the spare bedroom and turn it into detailing central.

That accomplished, you will need some basic furniture, equipment, and supplies to get the business rolling. Among your most critical needs are:

- **A desk and a comfortable office chair:** Do not even think about using a chair you have dragged in from the dining room, or about using the dining room table as a desk, for that matter. Office superstores and IKEA® businesses carry stylish, yet reasonably priced, office furniture. If you are really on a budget, scour thrift stores and online listings such as **www.craigslist.org** and The Freecycle Network (**www.freecycle.org**) for bargains. But do not skimp on your chair; comfort is crucial. A filing cabinet is also a good idea for overflow paperwork from your desk.

- **A computer system and software:** You will definitely need a computer with sufficient memory to run programs such as Intuit® QuickBooks or Microsoft® Excel, as well as to answer e-mail generated by visitors to your Web site. If you already have a computer or laptop, repurpose it for the business to minimize your start-up costs.

- **Business phone line:** You will definitely need a line used only for the business. Do not try to make your home land-line or personal cell phone do double duty. Install a second phone line in your office or get a family plan for your cell phone and add a second phone. In today's world, voice-mail is absolutely necessary, although you can use an answering machine to pick up calls if you prefer.

- **Office supplies:** You will need the basics, from pens and paper to file folders and sticky notes. Use what you already have around the house to save some scratch.

- **Digital camera:** If you do not have a camera at hand, purchase one because you will want to post photos of the vehicles you detail on your Web site to reel in new customers.

## Processing payments

You will need a couple more things to rake in all the dough in your detailing dreams. Unless you plan to operate on a cash-only basis — which is not uncommon among detailers — the first thing you will need is a merchant account, which is an electronic clearinghouse that tells you whether a buyer has sufficient credit available to buy from you or enough cash in a bank account to cover a debit-card purchase. Several service fees are associated with merchant accounts, from a fixed transaction fee (often 1.25

percent to 4 percent per transaction), to a processing fee (about 20 cents per transaction), a monthly minimum fee, a charge-back processing fee, and more. The good news is that merchant account rates are fairly competitive, so search "merchant accounts" on the Internet and see what turns up. Your neighborhood bank quite likely offers small-business merchant account services, so it is worth a call or a foray online to check out the terms and fees.

Merchant accounts require special credit-card-processing equipment to do their magic. In addition to a point-of-sale (POS) terminal, which is the little box where you swipe the credit card to transmit data, you will need a receipt printer. A commercial or home-based shop generally should have a standard desktop POS terminal and receipt printer sitting right on the counter. You can save some cash and counter space by investing in POS software that turns your computer printer into a receipt printer. Check out the QuickBooks POS software add-on, which works with its general accounting software (**www.quickbooks.com**).

If you do not need stand-alone POS equipment, look into a mobile payment terminal instead. These handheld devices require wireless Internet access or a connection through an Internet-enabled cell phone. In some cases, the devices have a receipt printer built right in, making it quick and easy to clear transactions. A couple of systems to investigate include the First Data™ FD50 (**www.firstdata.com**), with its built-in printer; and the PowerSwipe® attachment (available at **www.creditcardstore.com**), which works with many brands of Internet-enabled cell phones, including Nextel. But you will need a wireless receipt printer to use the PowerSwipe.

Finally, these days it is becoming more common for retail merchants of all types to accept PayPal, an online checkout system, as a payment option. It will cost you a little more to use PayPal versus a merchant account, and your cash is not deposited instantly, but you can avoid the hassle of real-time swiping and clearing because the customer will already have a vetted and approved account set up. He or she just has to transfer the funds to your PayPal account. This might be a good option for a detailer who does a lot of corporate or fleet work and sends invoices for his or her services. For more information on how to accept PayPal payments, go to **www.paypal.com**.

Although this chapter focuses more on home-based and mobile businesses, you certainly can use any of the information discussed here when setting up a shop in a commercial building. You will find additional information about shop offices and how to find and lease a facility in the next chapter. In the meantime, look again at the start-up checklist in this chapter, which you can use when trying to figure out how much start-up money you need. If you start as a home-based venture with no equipment, tools, or products at all, and you are conservative, you can get pretty much everything you need for about $2,000 to $3,000. Add in an entry-level detailing trailer if you are going mobile, and you will be closer to the $5,000 to $8,000 range. In the grand scheme of things, that is an extremely low price to set up a self-sustaining business and, with any luck, you can pay for whatever you need out of personal savings. You might need financial assistance possibly because you want higher-end tools and products, you want to purchase a franchise, or you want to establish a brick-

and-mortar business. *You will find a discussion of potential funding sources and strategies in Chapter 12.*

# Chapter 7

## Car Love

Chances are, if you are a committed motor head or devoted car enthusiast, you may have detailed your personal vehicles many, many times. Because you soon will be detailing for money as well as love, you may find it helpful to take a methodical approach to the process. Doing so will streamline your detailing activities, as well as help you detail customers' cars in the most efficient and cost-effective way possible. This chapter provides step-by-step instructions for a complete car detailing that you can tweak or adapt to meet your own high specifications.

# The Customer Meet-and-greet

One of the most important steps in the detailing process is the initial meeting. A 10-minute discussion with your valued customers will help you understand their expectations, which in turn will help you meet those expectations flawlessly. A brief customer meeting also gives you the perfect opportunity to up-sell the additional services you offer, such as paintless dent repair (PDR) or a paint sealant application, all of which will help you make more money on the sale.

Up-sell only after you have inspected the vehicle, not when the customer is on the phone. That way, you can point out areas that could use some extra attention, such as a scratched bumper or a dinged quarter panel, and explain what you can do to take care of them. This also shows that you are knowledgeable about the vehicle. Generally speaking, people who love their vehicles appreciate the opportunity to have all the work done at the same time and likely will give you the go-ahead.

You even can make extra money on detailing and repair services you do not offer, such as window tinting or bumper repainting. Just line up a few local auto-service providers you can trust, and you will always have someone on standby to handle whatever comes up. Say, for example, you have a detailing customer whose bumper is significantly scratched from kissing parking barriers too many times. If you have already established a relationship with a nearby collision shop or mobile auto-painting business, you can quote the price of bumper repainting to your customer — along with a 10 percent markup for your trouble, of course — and the customer probably will be happy to leave both the detailing and the repainting in your capable hands.

## CASE STUDY: MAKE THE CUSTOMER HAPPY

Anthony Flammia
Gia's Detailing of Long Island Inc.
P.O. Box 5350
Miller Place, NY 11764
Phone: 631-473-1217
E-mail: customerservice@giasmobile.com
Web site: www.giasdetailing.com

Anthony Flammia was born and raised in Long Island, New York, and has owned Gia's Detailing of Long Island since 2004.

Flammia first became involved in the detailing industry as a child in the mid 1970s. His father, Stuart, started an auto-reconditioning business called Stuart's Simonizing of Huntington in 1959, and the younger Flammia learned how to care for various types of vintage automobiles, boats, RVs, motorcycles, and aircraft, as well as modern vehicles. Although in 1984 he fulfilled a lifelong dream to become a police officer with the New York Police Department, Flammia continued to work with his father in the family business.

"This business is in my blood," he said.

As an industry expert, Flammia has consulted with various businesses to help set up profitable detail shops on both the dealership and local levels. Most recently he consulted with Pronto Wash USA, a global leader in eco-friendly car washing and detailing. As part of the job, he helped raise the profitability of the average ticket price, established training programs and protocols for franchisees, and established a winter wash program suitable for the cold climates of the Northeast that allows technicians to use a low-pressure wash system. In addition, he worked with various manufacturers on developing an eco-friendly wash to remove heavy contaminants on the surface of vehicles during the Northeast's harsh winters. He also tested various steam machines for washing vehicle exteriors, then established suitable washing procedures.

Since retiring from the NYPD's elite Highway Patrol Motorcycle unit in

2004, Flammia took over his father's business and renamed it. His exclusive mobile-detailing company caters to an upscale clientele who own homes valued above $600,000 and have annual incomes at $150,000 and above. His services include auto detailing, paintless dent removal, paint touch-up, windshield repair, mold remediation, exclusive show-car detailing, and more. He also offers a full day of detailing, in which technicians spend eight hours on a single car. Prices range from $600 to $1,200, and the exclusive service features Swissvax, a premier wax from Switzerland.

Flammia credits his father with teaching him so much about the detailing business.

"Dad was a tough teacher," he said. "He kept telling me how to do things right and emphasized doing the right thing by the customers. I walked away from the business numerous times when I was young, but I always kept my hand in the business full-time while I was employed with the police department."

When Flammia took over his father's business, he promptly began promoting his new business via a Web site. He also invested in a professional-looking detailing trailer and complete uniforms for every employee. The uniforms, he says, go far in establishing the professionalism he expects in his business.

On average, Flammia uses at least eight different products to get a detailing job done right. The equipment he uses on a daily basis includes a properly set-up trailer, a buffing wheel, clay, compound, polish, waterless wash, steam machine, carpet extractor, commercial vacuum, and microfiber towels.

Because water conservation has become a hot topic in the detailing industry, Flammia has made some adjustments in his detailing regimen, beginning with using a steam machine to clean and deodorize vehicle interiors. He uses the same equipment to wash vehicle exteriors. According to his research, this technique is a viable alternative even in colder climates.

Overall, Flammia credits his personal work ethic for his success, bolstered by the excellent customer service his business offers and the lessons he learned from his father, who ran his own business for 45 years. He offers this advice to new detail shop owners:

- Work hard and focus on providing customer service that makes the customer happy.

- Be prepared to invest a good deal of money to set up a mobile or fixed location properly.

- Have a professional appearance. This applies to both the owner and the technicians.

- Hire people who exhibit good personal grooming, have good conversational skills, and maintain their own vehicles well, as these are reflections on the company.

- Keep your employees happy and pay them well. "That means paying a salary plus commission," Flammia said.

- Price your services well, but adjust prices when the market or situation warrants. "When gas prices go up, my prices have to increase, too," he said.

Gas prices are not the only thing that can affect the price of detailing services. The condition of a vehicle's exterior paint, its color, and its nameplate all can influence the price. In addition, factors such as whether the vehicle has been exposed to a commercial car wash and how much time is needed to bring the car back to a near-new state may influence the charge.

Although Flammia does work with both individuals and retailers, he prefers not to do dealer work.

"I don't work with dealers because they want the service for almost nothing," he said.

Instead, Flammia prefers to focus on other valued customers, who he says tend to notice the attention his crew pays to interior details, such as door jams, trunk lids, and windows.

"But there is no doubt that the most important part of the job is whatever makes the vehicle look its best," he said. "In most cases, that is the exterior of the car and how shiny it looks after a professional detail job."

# The Car Detailing Process

Start a detail by cleaning the interior first. If you do the exterior first, or if your employees try to detail the interior and exterior simultaneously, it is practically guaranteed that whatever dirt and dust has been stirred inside will end up contaminating the freshly washed exterior. However, if engine detailing will be part of the services provided, it is usually advisable to make that the very first step, as the engine compartment often is the dirtiest part of the vehicle.

Always have a good supply of clean, white towels on hand. Make sure you have a receptacle nearby for collecting the soiled towels to keep your shop clean and tidy. Chamois are a good, lint-free option for wiping painted surfaces, but microfiber towels are the answer to drying wet cars.

| THE INTERIOR DETAILING PROCEDURE |
|---|
| ▶ Remove the floor mats and vacuum them thoroughly. Use a stiff nylon brush and an appropriate stain remover on spots. Different stain removers are available to treat protein stains, tar/grease, tannins (coffee and tea), red dye, rust, and pet stains. Shampoo the mats and use a pressure washer (if not extremely dirty) or carpet extractor (if very dirty) to force out the soapy water. Set the mats aside in a visible location so you will not forget to replace them later. |
| ▶ Bag up any loose items from inside the car, as well as any items in the glove box and console. Always leave the bags inside the car so you do not misplace them. |
| ▶ Use a blower to blow dirt out of hard-to-reach areas, including under the seats and in crevices, vents, door pockets, and cup holders. |
| ▶ Vacuum the carpet quickly to remove all loose debris, then do a second, more thorough vacuuming of the carpet and upholstery. Pay particular attention to removing pet hair. |

| ▶ | Flip up folding seats or take out removable back seats, blow out dirt, then vacuum beneath them. |
|---|---|
| ▶ | Apply spot-remover chemicals to the carpet and fabric upholstery. Scrub with a stiff brush. |
| ▶ | Remove all ashtrays. Wash, dry, and replace them. |
| ▶ | Collect the chemicals, cleaning tools, and towels you will need for the interior detail, and get into the driver's seat. |
| ▶ | Clean the headliner using a towel moistened with spray cleaner. Do not saturate the headliner, because that can loosen the glue that holds it in place. Work about halfway toward the back. You will clean the other half when you move to the passenger side of the car. |
| ▶ | Clean the trim around the windshield within arm's reach, as well as the door trim. |
| ▶ | Clean the sun visor and rearview mirror. |
| ▶ | Clean the dashboard and around the knobs and buttons of the instrument panel. Apply the cleaning solution to your scrubby pad or brush rather than directly to the dashboard's precision parts to avoid damaging the finishes. Dry carefully. |
| ▶ | Scrub the steering wheel, steering column (including all knobs and levers), center console, and arm rests. |
| ▶ | Shampoo the carpets and remove the residue with a carpet extractor. Use paper or plastic mats to protect carpet that remains damp after extraction. |
| ▶ | Wipe the foot pedals with cleaner, but do not use rubber-dressing products on them because they will become slippery. |
| ▶ | Shampoo/clean the upholstery using fabric shampoo. Use the extractor once and repeat if necessary. With leather, always do a patch test first in an inconspicuous area to test for colorfastness and stain resistance and to make sure the product does not strip the leather's finish. On vinyl upholstery, use the appropriate cleaning spray and scrub. |
| ▶ | Run a clean, dry towel over the upholstery to remove as much moisture as possible. |
| ▶ | Shampoo the seat belts and use spot remover, if necessary, then clean the buckles. |

| | |
|---|---|
| ▶ | Wipe the door panel and spray all-purpose cleaner around the door jam and edge. Wipe dry. Use cotton swabs or other small detailing tools on any dirt or stubborn stains that remain. |
| ▶ | Leave the door open to air out the interior thoroughly and to speed up drying time. |
| ▶ | Repeat on the front passenger side of the vehicle. |
| ▶ | Move to the passenger-side back seat with the appropriate supplies in hand. |
| ▶ | Clean the rest of the headliner on the driver's side as far as the back window. |
| ▶ | Clean the rear deck. |
| ▶ | Wipe the back seats, then shampoo/clean them, as appropriate. |
| ▶ | Wipe the side panels, the back of the front seat, and the headrest. |
| ▶ | Shampoo the carpet and door panel. |
| ▶ | Wipe the door jam. |
| ▶ | Repeat on the front passenger side of the vehicle. |
| ▶ | Move back to the front driver's side and apply dressing and/or leather conditioner to all leather, vinyl, and plastic parts. |
| ▶ | Spray window cleaner on the windows within reach and wipe dry. Give the windows a final polish with a dry cloth to remove any streaks and spots that may have been left behind. |
| ▶ | Repeat on the back driver's side, back passenger side, and front passenger side. |
| ▶ | Deodorize the interior. |

## THE EXTERIOR DETAILING PROCEDURE

| | |
|---|---|
| ▶ | Use a pressure washer to wet the entire vehicle. |
| ▶ | Open the hood and wash the engine, starting at the top. |
| ▶ | Apply engine degreaser and scrub with a brush; rinse thoroughly with the pressure washer. |

▶ Blow excess water out of the engine and engine compartment using an air compressor.

▶ Spray water-based dressing on the engine, then close the hood. Let it dry shiny.

▶ Wet the wheels, wheel wells, and jams using the pressure washer.

▶ Apply wheel and tire cleaner on one side of the car. Scrub with the appropriate brushes and rinse.

▶ Move to the other side and repeat.

▶ Use a bug sponge to scrub bugs off the front grill, fender, license plate, and the back of the side mirrors.

▶ By hand, wash the exterior with car shampoo, using a natural sea sponge or mitt. Start at the top and work in small sections to avoid recontamination, then rinse with the pressure washer.

▶ Dry with a chamois or lint-free towel. Because water contains microscopic minerals that can scratch the vehicle's finish or eat away at the surface, do not allow water to dry on the paint.

▶ Remove road-tar spray, if present, using a product formulated for the job, then wipe off.

## THE TRUNK DETAILING PROCESS

▶ Open the trunk and remove the spare if it or its compartment is dirty.

▶ Remove loose items and bag the smaller items; set aside.

▶ Remove the carpet liner, if possible. If not, you will have to shampoo it in place.

▶ Vacuum the entire trunk compartment.

▶ Apply spot remover and/or degreaser to the liner and scrub with a stiff brush. Wipe with a clean towel or use the extractor, if necessary.

▶ Clean the trunk lid.

▶ Spray cleaner on the trunk jam and wipe.

▶ Shampoo the carpet liner; extract the liquid.

| | |
|---|---|
| ► | Wipe all sidewalls of the trunk. |
| ► | Use the pressure washer to clean the spare if you have re-moved it from the trunk. Spray it with dressing, wash it with the pressure washer, dry it, and replace it in the trunk. |
| ► | Spray dressing on a towel and dress any remaining rubber, in-cluding the weather stripping, as well as vinyl and plastic parts. |
| ► | Deodorize the trunk and replace the loose items. |

## THE PAINT TREATMENT PROCESS

| | |
|---|---|
| ► | Clay the vehicle by hand, if necessary, to remove paint over-spray, surface rust, rail dust fallout, and/or other environmental contaminants. Rub in a circular motion. |
| ► | Use a high-speed buffer and the appropriate rubbing compound and cutting pad to remove major or minor scratches and oxida-tion, if necessary (if not necessary, you will simply polish and apply a wax or sealant product, as described later). Work in 2-by-2-foot sections, starting at the hood and moving counter-clockwise around the vehicle. Keep the speed at 1,000 to 1,200 RPM. Clean your pad frequently during the buffing process. |
| ► | Use a buffer, polishing pad, and swirl-removal polish to remove swirls and compound scratches, and restore the shine by using the same techniques just described. Fix small scratches by hand in tight places, such as under the door handles. |
| ► | Apply wax or sealant by hand, using an applicator pad or an orbital waxer. You can use any one of several orbital or dual-action waxers on the market. |

## THE FINISHING TOUCHES

| | |
|---|---|
| ► | Wipe all trim, tires, and bumpers again to remove excess dressing. |
| ► | Polish chrome, including emblems and tailpipes. Steel wool is especially useful for this purpose. |
| ► | Clean the edges and interior of the gas-cap compartment. |
| ► | Check for compound polish or wax that may have been left in cracks and crevices, and remove it with a detail brush. |

| | |
|---|---|
| ▶ | Place the floor mats in trunk. |
| ▶ | Make a final inspection of the entire vehicle, then drive it into natural light or roll up the shop door to check for streaks on the windows, or sealant or wax that was not completely removed. Apply a little elbow grease to correct any imperfections. |

This is a lot to remember, even if you are an old hand at detailing your own vehicles. Customers will expect perfection when they leave their rides in your hands, so it is important to do the most competent, thorough job possible on every vehicle. *To help make sure that happens, this book condensed all the information discussed above into a one-page checklist on the companion CD-ROM that you can use as you work.*

If you are new to detailing and would like a little video help to set you on the path to detailing success, you will find plenty of instructional videos and other detailing 411 on the Internet. AutoGeek Ultimate Motor Community (**www.autogeek.com**), Meguiar's (**www.meguiars.com**), and many product manufacturers offer free instructional videos right online, while suppliers such as Detail Plus and Rightlook sell useful training videos targeted at the novice detailer, as well as hands-on training in detailing, PDR, paint touch-up, vehicle graphics, interior repair, and windshield repair.

# Chapter 8

## Buffer Zone

Now that you have a good idea of the many under-the-hood activities that go into establishing a detailing business, it is time to turn your attention to finding a place to do all that washing, polishing, and claying. For detailers who do not intend to take their show on the road, that means leasing or buying a building.

All detailers will have different building needs. Some prefer to have a facility with bays (service areas) and hydraulic hoists, while others just need an open area, such as a warehouse, that has good lighting and plenty of space to work. The most frugal entrepreneurs just need to clean out their garages to make room for their pressure washer and clay bars. Just be sure that no matter where you detail, you have sufficient room to store all your equipment and chemicals in one place.

This chapter primarily deals with the 411 you need to lease and set up a brick-and-mortar facility.

# Building Basics

Finding a brick-and-mortar facility to lease or buy is not much different from looking for a new home. You simply find a listing agent who handles commercial real estate, then have him or her line up for your inspection a variety of garages or other buildings you can convert. These days, you also can do some of the legwork yourself by searching the Internet with terms such as "auto detailing building," "automotive business for sale," or "commercial garage for lease," along with the name of your city, and seeing what turns up. But you probably will find it more efficient and a better use of your time to leave the job in the hands of an experienced commercial real estate broker or rental agent. *Choosing a site that has a proper drain system is discussed in Chapter 12.*

There are other important benefits to using commercial real estate brokers. They will have valuable inside information about the market they serve, from which parts of town are well populated and prosperous — which, hopefully, will confirm your own market-research findings — to local zoning and tax laws that could impact your business. They will be able to identify where your competition is located so you can keep a respectful distance. They also will be able to tailor your building search to the areas that best fit your budget and needs. Finally, they can handle details such as arranging title searches, helping secure financing, acting as an intermediary between the seller and yourself, and closing the sale. Deciding whether to buy or lease should be one of the first issues you discuss with your broker because the decision will help narrow the pool of available properties. If you are not sure which way to go, your broker can advise you about that, too.

Buying a commercial building gives you tax advantages, though few detailers can afford to buy one. Assuming that the local zoning allows a business such as yours, you also will be free to modify the building to suit your needs, and you can control the overhead costs. When you lease, you must contend with a landlord who will have a say in any modifications you need to make, and you will be at his or her mercy when basic building repairs are required. If you do not want to worry about building maintenance, then a lease might be for you. Just be sure to negotiate favorable terms up front so you do not get any unpleasant surprises later. Ask your attorney to look over any leasing contracts and addenda before you sign on the bottom line — or you could find yourself in more than just soapy water down the road.

## Types of facilities

Although fixed-location detailers typically set up shop in stand-alone buildings, they also may lease space from other auto-related businesses, including auto malls that offer services such as oil changes, auto glass repair, and brake replacement; auto dealerships; and car washes. This type of location is advantageous because customers are already accustomed to going to such a site for all of their auto-related services, so it would be logical for your auto-related business to be there, too. Also, as mentioned earlier, large, open buildings like warehouses can make great detailing hubs.

While you are hunting for a facility, keep an eye out for defunct auto repair or collision shops, oil change businesses, and tire stores that might be available for lease or purchase. These types of buildings may already have in place the bays and hoists, picture windows, and storage areas you need. Note that although hydraulic lifts are not necessary, they do make undercarriage detailing possible. These types of buildings also may already have a sewer system with a sand trap and oil separator, which are required by the Environmental Protection Agency (EPA) and other regulatory agencies for removing sludge from discharged water. The existence of such a system in working condition is definitely a plus because it tends to be expensive if installed new.

Although an operational sand trap and oil separator may be enough to get you prepped to purchase, do sufficient due diligence before making a deal. Research the business thoroughly to find out exactly why it is shuttered. If it is because the location was bad (read: did not generate enough business), the operation was mismanaged, or the taxes were too high, you might want to walk away. Use the Internet to research the company and the community to get a read on what problems might have plagued the defunct business.

Finally, be careful about taking over an abandoned gas station. In the mid-1980s, Congress decreed that owners of businesses with underground storage tanks (USTs) upgrade, replace, or close them as a way to address threats to our country's groundwater. According to the EPA, more than 101,000 UST cleanups have not been completed. No doubt some of them belong to gas stations, which means that if you buy or lease such a business, you would be responsible for the tank cleanup or replacement, as well as the petroleum brownfield (the ground contaminated by petroleum) that the gas station sits on. Forty states have UST funds to help with remediation, but you really do not need that kind of hassle when you are trying to start a new business — not to mention, you may reside in a state that has no funds. For more information about USTs, visit the EPA's site at **www.epa.gov/oust**. Regardless, it is probably best to steer clear of old gas stations.

## Lease basics

When you start searching for a building, you are likely to encounter several different types of leases — some of which, depending on your budget, may be deal breakers. The most common types of commercial leases include:

- **Gross lease:** You make the monthly lease payment, and your landlord covers virtually everything else, including the utilities, taxes, repairs, and maintenance.

- **Closed-end (or net) lease:** You pay rent plus a portion of the landlord's operating expenses, including maintenance, taxes, and utilities.

- **Triple-net lease:** You pay every cost related to the building's use (a landlord's dream lease).

- **Shopping-center lease:** You may encounter this type of lease if you lease a building on a parcel of land (outlot) that is part of a shopping center or mall, or possibly in an auto mall. In a shopping center lease, your rent is tied to the square footage of your space, and you generally must pay for maintenance of common areas. And — you might want to sit down for this one — you must fork over a percentage of your gross receipts each month. That might not be the first thing you want to do, but if you have an outstanding location with plenty of traffic and visibility, such a high cost may be worth considering.

No matter which type of lease you are presented with, run (do not walk) to your attorney's office with the paperwork clutched in hand. There are too many variables in a commercial lease to try to navigate this alone. Always have your attorney review the contract before you sign.

## Taking center stage

When you are making that important decision about where to establish your new shop, always give location serious consideration. Choose a building on a busy, well-lit, well-maintained street with easy access from both directions, and test its accessibility by driving past the building yourself. Neither foot traffic nor parking are especially important when it comes to a detailing shop, as most services are either rendered on the spot (express detailing) or by appointment over a period of several hours (full-service detailing). It is a good idea, however, to select a location that is surrounded by other busy retail establishments or restaurants. Simply being in the same orbit as other successful businesses helps build visibility for yours, even if diners or shoppers are not in the mood for an express detailing at that particular moment.

Speaking of other businesses, make sure they are keeping their property as clean and well maintained as you will keep yours. If you locate your sparkling new or remodeled facility next to run-down businesses or in an area that is past its prime, that will not reflect well on your own enterprise and may keep customers away.

# The Well-equipped Detail Shop

Before negotiations progress to the point where you are signing a lease, you need to make sure the facility you have selected is suitable for your needs. Generally speaking, a start-up detailing shop will need about 2,000- to 2,500-square feet to accommodate three vehicle bays plus a wash bay for prepping vehicles before detailing; a waiting room with a counter and retail-product displays; a storage room for products, tools, and a washer and dryer; a small manager's office; and a unisex restroom. By comparison, a six-vehicle-bay shop with the same features would need about 4,000 square feet, and a 15-bay business — something to aspire to later — might need 7,000 square feet or more. You must set up the bays so there is sufficient room for several people to work on the vehicles from all sides at the same time and, of course, products and tools must be within easy reach. About 75 percent of the facility should be designated as the work area.

As you know from Chapter 6, you can outfit your new detailing shop by purchasing all kinds of fun automotive tools and products. But you may find it easier and more cost-effective to purchase a detailing system that includes much of the basic equipment and products you need to start detailing right away. One such system is offered by Detail Plus Car Appearance Systems (**www.detailplus.com**), which includes chemical workstations with detailing chemicals, compounds and waxes, a wet/dry vacuum, a soil extractor, and matching work carts. You can find sample layouts for two-, three-, and four-bay detailing shops on the Web site to see how everything works together.

Speaking of outfitting your shop, you need to give your waiting area special attention. In addition to having comfortable seating (no plastic chairs, please), the waiting area should have a wall-mounted TV, preferably with cable service; complimentary bottled water and coffee (and someone to make sure the coffee keeps coming); and a table with up-to-date reading material. A small play area for kids and Wi-Fi service are definite pluses if you can swing them. The waiting room and its accompanying restroom must be kept in pristine condition, which means you either will have to divide cleanup duty among your staff (assuming you have staff, that is) or hire a company to come in to service the area on a regular basis.

Finally, if you plan to offer retail car-care products — and you should, to generate another income stream — you will need to carve out a space for a well-stocked product area. You can purchase attractive wall-mounted shelving units at big-box stores such as The Home Depot that will keep products within easy reach for browsing while customers wait for their rides to be spiffed up. In addition to cash-and-carry products such as dashboard cleaners or chamois buffers, consider offering car-themed gift items such as key chains, sport bottles that fit into vehicle cup holders, or even flash drives emblazoned with automotive emblems. These types of products, known in advertising circles as "trinkets and trash," usually are very affordable, and you can mark them up to provide a tidy add-on profit for your business. You can find many advertising specialty companies on the Internet or listed in the Yellow Pages.

## Sign of success

Lots of cars parked in and outside your detailing shop certainly will announce your presence in the community, but the best way to make a statement is with a large, well-lit exterior sign that is clearly visible from the street. If you happen to snag a coveted corner location where your business is visible from two streets, two signs would efficiently advertise that you are open for business. The sign should give the name of your business in large letters and also can include your logo. *This is something you will read about in Chapter 10.* A backlit sign that remains lit even when the business is closed for the day is usually the best choice, even if your electricity bill is a bit higher.

Erecting that sign should be high on your priority list, not the last thing you do before officially opening the business. For one thing, your community may have restrictions on the size, color, or placement of exterior signage. This is particularly true in communities with historic districts. You need to know this as soon as possible so you can mull over your options. Talk to your landlord or the city clerk to find out what the restrictions, if any, may be.

Your sign can start to build buzz in the community about your new business before it ever opens. So once you are clear about the local ordinances, find a local company that manufactures, designs, and installs commercial signage, and get the process started. You also will need interior signage for the waiting room to inform customers about services, prices, and hours. Matching interior and exterior signage will give your business a more professional and coordinated look.

# Mobile Detailing Solutions

As you know from Chapter 6, the most cost-effective way to blast into the detailing universe is by launching a mobile business. Although you will have to invest in a mobile detailing trailer and possibly a truck or other vehicle to tote your business around, you will avoid building-overhead costs, which tend to eat up a significant portion of a site-based detailer's monthly revenues.

Mobile detailers are not completely off the hook: You still need some type of storage facility for your rig when it is not in use. That is because the city fathers and your neighbors are unlikely to appreciate seeing your Mo's Mobile Detailing trailer parked in front of your house or in your driveway every day from 6 p.m. to 8 a.m. You are going to have to find another place to stash your rig when it is enjoying some downtime.

The perfect solution is to rent a storage unit at a self-store facility. A 10-by-20-foot unit, which is about the size of a one-car garage, is all you need to store your detailing trailer, although if you want to park your truck inside, too, you will need a larger unit. Self-storage units usually are climate-controlled and totally secure, and they have drive-up access 24/7 for convenience. Add some steel shelving along the walls to hold detailing products so they will not take up space in your own already-crowded garage.

## CASE STUDY: LOCATION AND CONVENIENCE

Jim Fitzpatrick
ProntoWash of Southern California
1048 Irvine Ave No. 723
Newport Beach, CA 92627
Phone: 949-257-8448
E-mails: jfitz@prontowash.com,
prontowash@msn.com

Jim Fitzpatrick grew up in Boston and came to car detailing via an education at the University of Notre Dame and a career with the pharmaceutical company that is now GlaxoSmithKline. He became an international business executive and eventually decided he wanted to live in Orange County, California, get off the airplane roller-coaster, and have a flexible work schedule that would give him the chance to raise a family.

One wife and two children later, Fitzpatrick has fulfilled his dream — and for the past few years has been a master franchisee for ProntoWash, a mobile system that uses biodegradable products and less than one pint of water per service. As a franchisee, he is free to develop his territory or own his own locations. He has opened and sold five locations and plans to own several more in the next three years.

Fitzpatrick's clientele at ProntoWash of southern California consists of the people who are visiting a shopping mall, office, airport, country club, or any other location where he can set up a point-of-service spot for his business.

"This clientele could also include the time-starved executive or busy soccer mom," he added. "Busy people in general are our target customers."

Convenience is the key business driver at ProntoWash of Southern California. For this reason, Fitzpatrick is careful to select what he calls "A" locations that are highly visible to people as they enter a public property, parking lot, or parking structure. The idea is to show them at a glance that they can multitask — perhaps visit the mall or leave a vehicle at the airport during a business trip — and have their car cared for properly at the same time. To increase visibility, he uses professionally designed signage and point-of-purchase materials to hook customers.

"This type of setup allows washing and detailing to be delivered conveniently at locations traditionally unavailable to the detailing industry," he said. "It's a great convenience, too, because we can offer an amenity that helps people repurpose their time — plus, there's no more waiting at the car wash or detail shop."

Fitzpatrick focuses on express and maintenance detailing.

"This is the sweet spot for us in terms of time and money," he said. "The cost is from $99 to $149 for a car with one to two hours of service time. However, over time we have added services that meet our company's eco requirements while enhancing the convenience of the service."

In fact, one thing that attracted Fitzpatrick to ProntoWash's business model was its emphasis on water conservation and the elimination of water run-off. Once he fixed all city permitting issues, Fitzpatrick started promoting the business in two ways.

"First, when I opened a location at an office building or shopping mall, I negotiated for the most visible and convenient location," he said. "Then I developed programs that were of most value for the customer. For instance, we developed VIP programs that encouraged frequency of service and offered value to clients."

He even overcame the challenges associated with water use on the job.

"I believe water is the new oil, and the next wars will be fought over it," he said. "So I had to spend a tremendous amount of time and energy attending meetings, educating, and developing relationships with water districts, cities, state water control boards, and so on to promote the water conservation and no-run-off benefits of the business model I use. I won that round, and now a nationwide green movement is emphasizing sustainability criteria, so my business model definitely is in style."

One thing he definitely could have used in those formative years was a mentor or two. Although over time he did develop a few mentors he could count on, and he worked hard to develop additional industry relationships, there are things he would have done differently if he had strong mentors.

"I was a bit naïve in those days and believed I could overcome anything," he said. "But this was my first business, so I had no idea what I didn't know. I probably would have done what I did anyway, but a mentor would have helped me go in with my eyes wide open."

Now that he is in a position to be a mentor himself, he frequently passes on advice to those who want to open their own car detailing businesses.

"Figure out a good reason why [you want to do this]," he said. "Find some mentors as soon as possible. Do a budget and recognize that you will need more money than your budget shows. This industry has a low level of capital and a low level of training, and while many can survive, few thrive. So get good business advice and make sure you're trained by one of the best in the industry."

Fitzpatrick says there are many things owners and managers can do to improve employee retention.

"I can talk about many things like respect, training, and all that, but I find that the one thing that keeps employees coming back enthusiastically is a high-volume business," he said. "If you cannot bring in the cars, you will not be able to retain good help. So when I hire a new employee, the main qualities I look for include standard criteria like attention to details, good grooming habits, and good communication skills. But I also set up some basic hurdles, like meeting me at a certain time or calling me at 11 a.m. on a certain day, as a way to validate that the person we are considering is reliable and will follow through on directions."

ProntoWash is focused primarily on retail, but the company also has some pilots in wholesale and licensing that use the company's services. Fitzpatrick prides himself on pricing jobs fairly for each of his customers.

"For the basic wash, wax and detailing services, we have a standard price," he said. "We deliver a specific service within a specific time for a specific price. Services like scratch removal or detailing in conditions outside the norm require a separate price quote. We calculate what the costs will be, then we look at how much time a service will take and what profit we would like to make to arrive at a fair price."

Because products can increase the cost of a detailing job, Fitzpatrick is trying to reduce the number of products he uses. He suggested using only a few products in different concentrations so one product can perform many functions. In addition, introducing steam can reduce or eliminate the need for other products. But no matter how products are used, Fitzpatrick knows a sparkling-clean vehicle is what brings customers back. But one particular vehicle feature receives special attention in his shop: the windows.

"No matter how well you do a detail, if you blow the windows, you blow the customer impression," he warned.

Fitzpatrick sees a healthy future for mobile detailing and expects the industry to adopt eco-detailing.

"This is not really the detailer's choice to make this happen," he said. "But code changes, drought conditions, and the like will require widespread eco-detailing to become a reality. My prediction is that the trend will start in California and move east. Then we'll see what happens from there."

# When You Are Home Alone

Home-based detailers do not have detailing rigs, but they do need a secure and discreet place to work their magic. An ideal detailing space for the home-bound detailer is a two-car garage, which typically is about 400 square feet. That gives you enough room to detail one car under cover, plus space to move around and organize your tools and equipment. If that is not enough space for your booming business and you happen to live outside the city limits and have enough acreage, you might find that a small pole barn or equipment shed would make a suitable alternative to a garage. The smallest shed or pole barn is usually around 20- by 30 feet (horses not included). You will have to erect it on a concrete foundation, however, and that can be *very* pricey.

Do remember, however, that even though you might be operating on your own property, you still have to respect local zoning ordinances, which may prohibit the operation of a commercial

business in a residential neighborhood. Check with your municipality to find out the rules. In addition, either a wastewater containment system or a legal connection to the sanitary sewer is a
must. *These are both discussed in Chapter 12.*

## Nontraditional locations

There are a few other places where you can ply your trade without racking up huge overhead costs. You may be able to negotiate with a car wash, auto dealership, or auto-service center to
carve out a little corner in their facility to serve as your detailing headquarters. The owners of such businesses often like the
idea of offering additional services but may not have the personnel to handle them. So try pitching yourself as a paying tenant,
or give them a percentage of your gross sales in exchange for
some space. You will not only land a professional environment
in which to work, but you are also bound to score a fair amount
of walk-up business from people who are visiting for other in-
house services.

No matter where you choose to do business, try to keep the facility costs down e. For example, if you are planning to open a
brick-and-mortar shop, initially lease or buy the smallest facility
that will suit your needs. That will keep your monthly expenses
down, which is important for a start-up business. You can always
trade up to a larger and pricier facility when your workload ex-
pands and your income increases. Having a spacious and well-
equipped place in which to work is one thing. In the next chapter,
you will read about the employees you may need to steer your
new detailing venture in the right direction.

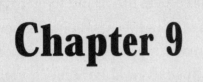

# Chapter 9

## Your Pit and Polish Crew

O ne of the great things about starting a car detailing business is that you can go it alone and start making money right from the first day. But make no mistake about it: The amount of money a lone ranger can earn is limited. You have only a certain number of hours in the day to wash and polish, after all; plus, you have to handle all the administrative tasks that go along with being a small-business owner — tasks that tend to be quite time-intensive.

Clearly, a desire to make more money will seem like a good reason to start hiring. But it is usually a better idea to start your business with just one person (yourself) on the payroll as a way to keep expenses and costs manageable. If you have sufficient start-up capital to open a bigger operation, or you become so booked up that you have to turn down lucrative contracts, such as corporate or auto dealer work, then you probably will need to consider bringing some help on board.

This chapter explores the types of employees you may need, where to find them, how to evaluate them, and what to pay them when you do track them down. But it bears repeating here: Try to keep the personnel roster small for as long as you can, or at least until you get a feel for the business and how much you reasonably can expect to earn. But the cost of hired help is not the only reason why. To be honest, personnel management is not easy. You have to provide strong leadership, deal with personality conflicts, manage schedules and employee requests for time off, and provide training, among other things. Also, being responsible for another person's livelihood is a rather sobering experience for a small-business owner who already has plenty of other things to worry about.

*If you are planning to have a one-person operation, feel free to flip ahead to the next chapter, which covers effective advertising strategies for detailers.* Otherwise, let us shift gears and start hiring.

# Taking a Shine to the Hired Help

Ask virtually any small-business owner what his or her biggest challenge is and the answer is likely to be "finding qualified help." As a business owner yourself, you are bound to encounter the same problem. But you will find it is not so much a problem of finding enough people to do the job you are offering as it is finding the right people.

The main types of employees you are likely to need are detailing technicians and a shop manager. Even a very small business such as yours can benefit from a shop manager, whose job is *not* to detail vehicles, but to keep the operation running efficiently.

The shop manager is responsible for everything from ordering chemicals and supplies to scheduling appointments and cashing out clients. The manager also may have a hand in employee management, reconciling the receipts, keeping tax records straight, and much more — in short, handling the basic retail and administrative tasks so you, the owner, can be freed up to pursue new business, market the operation, and even detail the cars.

Detailing technicians, on the other hand, are the pistons that make the detailing engine go. They wash and wax, buff and dress. But what technicians do not need to have is prior detailing experience. In fact, detailing experts recommend hiring conscientious workers with no detailing experience because that makes it easier to teach them how to work according to your specifications. People with prior detailing experience may have their own ways of doing things that do not mesh with yours, and that may cause friction.

Industry detailing expert RL "Bud" Abraham takes that caveat against hiring experienced detailers to new heights when he says that they are not trainable because of the procedures and quirks they have developed. For instance, they might be too heavy-handed with the buffer, causing damage to the clear coat, or they may use more products than are necessary, which drives up the materials cost. He also says that they might not be very good at what they do, or they would be in business for themselves. Neither is a situation you want to deal with in your fledgling business.

This is not to say that you never should hire an experienced detailer for your business. But when interviewing, try to get a feel for whether the candidate will take instruction well and seems open to suggestions. That way, you can get the benefit that person's experience while still being able to train him or her to detail the way you prefer.

While you are probably more likely to need full-time employees to assist you in a full-service business, do not overlook the advantages of hiring part-timers, too. Half-time or fractional employees can help during busy times, then can go home when the rush is over. They also can fill in for employees who are vacationing or sick.

## Mapping out your employee search

Because this is blue-collar, manual labor, detailing businesses tend to pay workers minimum wage or a little more. Although this sounds great in terms of the bottom line, it is actually detrimental when it comes to hiring people. The type of people who will be able to work for $7.25 an hour, which is the current federal minimum wage, probably will have little job experience and minimal education. But since it is entirely possible to teach someone who is bright and willing how to detail correctly, these characteristics are not necessarily a drawback. You will find that strength of character, a sense of commitment, and personal accountability are much more important traits for prospective employees.

Although you can advertise for help in the local newspaper or on Craigslist (**www.craigslist.org**), these are not necessarily the best places to hunt. Not only will you get an avalanche of responses that you have to wade through, but you probably will attract plenty of those experienced detailers mentioned earlier whom you might want to avoid. Instead, ask family and friends for referrals to people they know are looking for work. Mention at church or your golf league that you are in the market for reliable workers. Spread the word at your networking group. Contact the local community college or high schools that have an automotive vocational program and offer a paid internship opportunity. Participate in any "career day" activities the institution may hold. Post details about your job opportunities on community bulletin boards or cable TV job boards.

Whatever you do, keep looking for prospective employees on a continual basis. One of the down sides of the employment picture in this industry is that detailing employees tend to job-jump, often switching jobs to make an extra 5 or 10 cents an hour somewhere else. So continue to accept job applications even if you are not currently hiring so you have some potential employee leads on file when a vacancy occurs.

To keep the undesirable element out of the search, Abraham recommends requiring applicants to have a high school diploma, a driver's license and good driving record, and at least some experience doing anything other than detailing in the recent past. These requirements should help keep the truly unqualified people away from your door. And they may literally arrive at your door, looking for work. For this reason, one of the first tasks you should undertake is having a ready supply of job applications on hand. If you like, you can create a custom application, but it is much simpler to head to the local office supply store and purchase a pack of employment applications. Alternatively, if you have Microsoft® Office software, you can download a variety of application templates at no cost from **http://office.microsoft.com**.

It is also important to develop a job description on paper. This might sound crazy when it comes to a manual job such as detailing, but the fact is, detailing is hard work, and if you spell out the

exact responsibilities for the job, you will avert any future misun-
derstandings — plus, you may discourage those candidates who
do not want to work that hard.

## Holding an "auto meet"

Once you have identified potential candidates for your inaugu-
ral set of employees, start the interview process by calling them
for a pre-employment phone screening. Ask a little about their
background (including any detailing or other automotive experience) and try to get a feel for their personality. Someone who
is enthusiastic and friendly on the phone is likely to be a cooperative employee, so that person should go on your short list of
interview candidates. Do not talk to more than about four or five
people in any given round of prescreening and interviewing. If
you exceed that number, they might start to get mixed up in your
head, which will make it harder for you to make a decision.

After phone prescreening, you are ready to invite a few job seek-
ers in for a little talk in the shop if you are up and running, or in
a neutral location such as a restaurant if you do not yet have a
facility. Always prepare a list of questions to ask, and be ready
to jot down some notes while the person is talking to jog your
memory later. When a candidate arrives, present him or her with
a job application and a copy of the job description. Once the application has been completed, sit down with the prospect and try
to get to know him or her. In addition to asking about the person's availability and ability to handle the manual parts of a detailer's job, ask a few personal questions concerning education,
work history, interests, hobbies, and so on. But stay away from
personal identity questions, including questions about marital
status, offspring, political affiliation, and sexual orientation.

Under Federal Equal Opportunity Employment Commission (EEOC) regulations, it is illegal to ask such questions because they hold the potential for discrimination.

As part of the interview, be sure to collect a list of the candidate's references, or make sure there is a place on the application to note them. Phone a few of these people later, starting with the work references. The idea is to ascertain whether the information on the job application is correct. You may find, however, that the candidate's past employers may not be willing to do much more than verify employment, the dates of employment, and the ending salary because of the potential for a legal backlash. But employers often will at least tell you that a former employee is agreeable or friendly or cooperative, and this might be enough to help you determine whether the candidate would be a good fit on your team.

Also during the interview, discuss the job responsibilities and your expectations for the employee. Touch on topics such as punctuality, reliability, hours, and working conditions. It is not necessary to discuss pay or benefits (if any) at the first meeting, although if you have a really strong candidate, you might want to mention the wage to gauge his or her reaction. Normally, however, you should defer the wage discussion until you are ready to make an offer of employment.

Finally, give the employee a tour of your shop if it is up and running. If not, discuss its various departments, keeping in mind that the person may not have more than a nodding acquaintance with a car detailer's responsibilities and tools. Allow the candidate to ask questions about the job and working environment. It is fine to avoid answering direct questions about pay and benefits if you prefer not to divulge the information at that time.

## Crossing the finish line

Although you may make a pretty solid decision to hire someone on the strength of the job interview, hold off on making an offer until after you have phoned the candidate's references and collected enough information to verify that this person is a good choice. Once your mind is made up, the next step is to make an offer, either by phone or in person.

On the employee's first day of work, have him or her fill out IRS Form W-4, Employee's Withholding Allowance Certificate, so you know how much federal income tax to withhold from his or her pay. You can download the form at **www.irs.gov/pub/irs-pdf/fw4.pdf**. Likewise, check with your state's treasury or tax division to see whether a similar state form must be filed. If you happen to be doing business in one of the seven states that do not collect state individual income tax — Alaska, Florida, Nevada, South Dakota, Texas, Washington, and Wyoming — you can skip this step. *You will find a more detailed (no pun intended) discussion about taxes in Chapter 12.*

As an employer, you are also required to have new hires fill out Form I-9, which verifies a person's identity and employment eligibility. All U.S. employers are required to collect a completed form from all employees, both citizens and noncitizens. At the time the form is filled out, the employee must present two pieces of identification as part of the verification process. Acceptable proof of citizenship or eligibility to work includes a valid U.S. passport or permanent resident card, certified copy of a birth certificate, or social Security card. Be sure to tell the employee to bring along these documents on his or her first day of work.

The I-9 form must be kept on file in your business records for at least three years after the date of hire or one year after termination, whichever is later. The forms must be available for inspection by agents of the U.S. Citizenship and Immigration Services (USCIS) or U.S. Homeland Security, if requested. The form can be loaded in both English and Spanish at no cost at the USCIS Web site at **www. uscis.gov**. A complete list of the documents that are considered acceptable proof of identify can be found on the last page of the I-9.

## CASE STUDY: QUALITY WORK AT A REASONABLE PRICE

Bill Proestler
5-Star Car Wash & Detail Center
900 E. Travis Blvd.        520 Orange Dr.
Fairfield, CA              Vacaville, CA
Phone: 707-425-9274        707-448-9274
Web site: www.5starwash.com

Founded in 1998, 5-Star Car Wash & Detail Center has two bay area locations and employs 55 to 60 people between them. But owner Bill Proestler's commitment to making cars sparkle and shine was forged much earlier in his life. His first paying job at the age of 16 was at a car wash.

Proestler has had a busy life in between now and then. In addition to serving in the Air Force, he held a variety of engineering and management positions with major corporations. When he decided to return to the clean-car industry, he founded 5-Star as a full-service car wash with an attached detail shop. At the time, the detailing shop constituted only a small part of the business's overall revenue. Since then, the detailing side has grown and now accounts for 33 percent of business sales.

Although you can get a traditional car wash or a basic detailing at 5-Star, the business specializes in full-service car washes and detailing. Interior detailing services are priced in "à la carte" fashion, such as carpet cleaning without a car wash (at $39.99) and odor removal ($25). The idea is to allow customers to customize their services and hopefully encourage them to try new services.

5-Star also offers oxidation removal, scratch repairs, and sealants. Proestler is quick to point out that employees sell only what the customer actually needs and never attempt to oversell.

"We want our customers to return on another day," he said. "Avoiding the hard sell is the best way to make that happen."

5-Star's main clientele runs the gamut from students to CEOs. This range, combined with the area's diverse demographics, makes marketing somewhat challenging. In some cases, Proestler does target specific market segments, such as auto dealers, fleets, and charity groups, but notes that the majority of his detailing business comes from the general public.

Although he does welcome the masses, Proestler warn that a detailer never should go after the low end of the customer pool.

"It is always better to do quality work and charge a reasonable price," he said. "If a customer is not willing to pay for professional services, let him or her go to the other guy who is willing to charge low prices and probably provides 'low' service and has little industry knowledge. And do not be concerned about losing out to the competition — with that level of service, the other guy probably will not be around long, anyway."

Proestler says that location has played an important role in his business's success.

"We just built a $3.5 million facility in a prime location, so we are sure to attract good clientele," he said.

For this reason, he recommends scouting out an area carefully before settling on a building — plus, having a car wash on the premises is another good way to bring the right business into a detailing shop.

When hiring, Proestler interviews people from various backgrounds, but he does not necessarily look for previous detailing experience.

"Many times we interview people who claim they have worked as detailers in the past," he said. "We ask them to do a demo on an old car to see what they actually know. Most of the time, they do not know what they are doing."

The candidates who do pass the test become valued employees — and many of them have been with his company for more than 10 years.

"Turnover is very expensive, so we try to keep our employees happy," Proestler said.

On the service side, he selects the best of everything in terms of equipment and chemicals.

"Good equipment helps to save on labor costs, which runs $60 an hour in our shop," he said. "We also stay away from chemicals that are potentially harmful to employees or customers. A good supplier who has knowledge of the business and the product he or she sells can help you there. In fact, many suppliers have been detailers themselves and really understand the business. Also be sure to keep the on-shelf products simple, and don't carry two different products that do the same thing, because you can save money just stocking one."

As an experienced car wash and detailing-shop owner, Proestler has encountered numerous operational issues over the years. He offers the following advice to prospective business owners to help them avoid common start-up pitfalls: "Because the detailing business is more complicated than most people realize, study the business first to know what you are getting into. Since you absolutely must know how to perform the service well, get some hands-on training, and learn as much as you can about the processes, products, and equipment."

Proestler believes detailing will continue to be a viable business in the future, even though the cost of labor, insurance, and quality chemicals is going up fast and presents a challenge.

"Nevertheless, as long as there are cars on the road, I think the future is bright for detailers," he said.

# Taxing Matters

One of the really fun parts about having employees — besides refereeing during disagreements and trying to juggle extra work when someone calls in sick — is the tax burden they dump on you upon arrival. It is not their fault, of course; it is just Uncle Sam feeding his need for operational cash flow. But the fact remains that as an employer, you will be responsible for paying more than just an hourly wage, and you will have more paperwork to contend with for the privilege.

To begin with, you will have to withhold federal and possibly state income tax from your employees' pay. As you know from being a virtually lifelong taxpayer, there is a formula for calculating the rate, which is best left to an accountant who knows the law. You also will have to withhold FICA, which is the social security tax that stands for the Federal Insurance Contributions Act, and Medicare tax. All these taxes have to be sent in to the appropriate taxing authority on a quarterly basis. This is something else your accountant can do on your behalf, but for more information for your edification, consult IRS Publication 15, *Employer's Tax Guide*, and Publication 583, *Starting a Business and Keeping Records*, both of which can be downloaded from **www.irs.gov**.

But the fun really begins when you start ponying up the employer taxes, including the matching portion of FICA (6.2 percent in 2009); state unemployment tax, which varies by state; a self-employment tax on your own earnings, which equates to the other half of the social security tax that you much pay because you are self-employed; and FUTA, or the federal unemployment tax, which starts at 0.8 percent but could be as high as 6.2 percent if you are not required to pay state unemployment insurance tax. You can find out the damages by checking out the state unemployment tax chart at **www.toolkit.com**. Last but not least, you will be responsible for workers' compensation insurance, which is a mandatory type of insurance that covers medical care for workers who are injured on the job. The rate for that insurance varies by state.

All these taxes tend to make a new business owner hesitate, but they absolutely should not scare you away from hiring helpers if you need them, as they simply are an inescapable cost of doing business. It is a good idea to find an experienced accountant pronto to help you wade through these taxing waters.

## To benefit or not to benefit

Offering fringe benefits such as health insurance, paid vacations, sick days, and other perks will instantly endear you to your staff, but the reality is that you may not be able to afford to do so. According to the Discover Small Business Watch index, which measures economic confidence among U.S. small-business owners with fewer than five employees, 85 percent of small-business owners do not offer health benefits — and with good reason. This is directly attributable to the cost. The U.S. Department of Labor's Bureau of Labor Statistics claims that benefits, which may also include profit sharing and retirement accounts, account for an average cost per hour of 29.2 percent. Many small businesses, including detailers, simply cannot afford such towering expenses.

As mentioned earlier, there tends to be a lot of turnover among detailing-shop employees, so the benefit issue might be a moot point anyway. But you may be able to increase your retention rate by offering some types of benefits, such as one week of paid vacation after a year of employment, or a couple of personal days.

## Pumping up your staff

It might hurt to part with those extra benefits dollars, but improving your retention rate is definitely something to strive for. The reason is that the more turnover you have, the more training you have to do — and, of course, that really can put a crimp in your operational efficiency.

Detailers tend to have to do a fair amount of training, anyway. They have to pass along the tricks of the track to their staff to improve their detailing skills; they must introduce staffers to new products; and they must demonstrate proper use of tools, both to protect their employees and to protect customers' vehicles from their employees. Most training can be done right in-house. But if you personally feel that you lack some skill necessary to make your business successful, as in the case of a detailer who has never kept the books or an investor/owner who has never before detailed a car, you might want to schedule yourself for detail industry training. Companies such as Detail King offer training in their own facility, while RL "Bud" Abraham of Detail Plus Car Appearance Systems will bring his training program, buoyed by his 40-plus years of car-industry experience, right to your door.

In addition, many of the detailing-chemical companies offer training in the use of their products. In some cases, you may have to travel to the company's headquarters or training facility; in other cases, the manufacturer's representative may be able to give an on-site demonstration. Check out the Web sites of the products you want to use to see whether the companies offer complimentary training.

# Safety Measures

Speaking of chemicals: They might be great for cleaning and conditioning customers' rides, but they can be murder on detailing technicians' respiratory systems and skin. As an employer, it is your responsibility to provide employees with a safe working environment and protective gear, as appropriate. In particular, this means making sure employees have adequate hearing and eye protection, as well as keeping the work area well ventilated to reduce the chances of inhaling noxious fumes that ultimately can cause health problems.

Workplace safety is regulated by a government agency known as OSHA, after the Occupational Safety and Health Act of 1970. Companies with fewer than 10 employers are exempt from keeping records on job-site injuries and work-related illnesses, but that does not mean you are off the hook when it comes to workplace safety. To get an idea of what you can do to keep your employees (and customers) safe, go to the OSHA Web site at **www.osha.gov**. It offers a wide range of workplace safety materials on everything from slip-and-fall accidents to the handling of wastewater, which can help you create a safer working environment and cut down on the incidence of workers' comp claims in your company.

Some of the OSHA safety guidelines applicable to a detailing shop include:

- Report injuries immediately, no matter how minor, and even if it seems that medical attention is not necessary.

- Use the power of your legs, not your back, when lifting heavy objects, including heavy machinery.

- Keep the work area clean, and correct workplace hazards (fluid spills, etc.) to prevent injury.

- Maintain tools and other equipment to keep them in good working condition. Remove damaged or malfunctioning equipment from service immediately.

- Remove rings, necklaces, and other hazardous items before working with power equipment. Keep long hair tied back to keep it out of machinery.

# Contract Help

Before we close this chapter on employees, it is important to discuss the use of independent contractors (ICs) in a detailing business. According to the IRS, an IC is a person who provides goods or services to a business under the terms specified in a contract. ICs are not actually employees of your company, and they can be brought in and sent away on a whim as your work ebbs and flows — and you do not have to pay for unemployment claims. You do pay them an hourly wage or a fee per project, but they are responsible for withholding their own taxes. You also do not have to pay the employer's half of federal taxes or mandatory costs such as workers' compensation. Finally, you do not have to issue any year-end paperwork to them other than a simple 1099-MISC form that indicates the gross amount paid the previous year.

To a small-business owner, ICs probably seem like dream employees — but the IRS will not just allow you to arbitrarily classify your workers as ICs without good justification. The IRS has what it calls "common law rules" that define whether someone is an employee or an IC. The common denominator of these rules relates to the amount of control the employer has over the worker. Here are the criteria the IRS uses to determine a worker's status, as seen at **www.irs.gov**:

- **Behavioral:** Does the company control or have the right to control what the worker does and how the worker does his or her job?

- **Financial:** Are the business aspects of the worker's job controlled by the payer? These include things such as how the worker is paid, whether expenses are reimbursed, who provides tools/supplies, etc.

- **Type of relationship:** Are there written contracts or employee-type benefits (e.g. pension plan, insurance, vacation pay, etc.)? Will the relationship continue, and is the work performed a key aspect of the business?

If you can answer "yes" to any of these questions, you have an employee, not an IC, and you need to treat him or her as such because Uncle Sam takes a very dim view of employers who try to evade taxes by misclassifying workers as ICs rather than employees. If caught, such employers are liable for stiff penalties and fines — as much as one year in jail and up to $100,000 in fines

— plus, they will be subject to an invasive IRS audit that could result in back taxes, more fines, and more penalties. So the point is, tread lightly when it comes to the IC issue. An attorney who specializes in tax issues can advise you on how to proceed.

Alternatively, the IRS will be happy to set (or scare) you straight on the distinction between ICs and employees. Check out the Businesses section at **www.irs.gov** for the full story. While you are there, download a copy of IRS Publication 15-A, *Employers' Supplemental Tax Guide*.

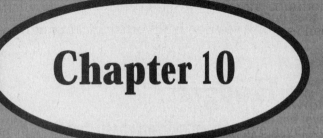

# Chapter 10

## Owner's Guide to Advertising

Once you have your business operations in place, you likely will be anxious to get those sprayers and buffers revved up so you can crank out beautifully detailed vehicles. However, there is another important task you must undertake to make sure you have a steady stream of customers racing to your shop. That task, of course, is to advertise so you can create demand for your services.

Back in Chapter 3, you read about the many things you can do to identify potential customers and target the market they move in. Now would be a good time to refer to the marketing plan you created so you can make some careful decisions about what you should do to bring customers to your shop. Because the amount of advertising a business owner does is, by necessity, driven by the amount of money he or she has stashed away, it is important to make extremely thoughtful decisions about how you spend that cash. So in this chapter, you will read about the types of advertising that tend to be most effective for car detailers, as well as how to go about launching your own advertising campaign.

# Setting the Budget

According to the Small Business Administration, fledgling entrepreneurs should allocate 2 to 5 percent of their gross monthly sales to advertising. At this point, when you do not have any monthly sales yet, that might seem like a hefty amount to come up when you could be spending the cash on a new extractor or other detailing tools and products. But just remember: That 5 percent can make a big difference in your level of success, so it is a non-negotiable point.

Let us say your first month's gross income is $3,000, which is doable for a new detailer. A 5 percent cut is only $150. Skim 5 percent off receipts of $5,000, and you are earmarking just $250. Now your task is to find the best way to spend that cash — which, admittedly, is not very much — to reach the most potential customers.

The types of advertising that tend to work best for car detailers are Yellow Pages' advertisements, brochures, postcards, fliers, door hangers, and coupons. Web sites also have their place in a detailer's advertising mix, but they are less a catalyst to spur spending than an information bank for people who are already interested in detailing services. You will notice that newspaper and magazine advertising are not included on this list. That is because ads in print mediums tend to be expensive and must be repeated many, many times to make an impression on the reading public. In addition, the print news industry is undergoing a metamorphosis because more people are getting their news and information online at no cost. For this reason, you probably should avoid print advertising at this time.

Another way to advertise your business that taps into the power of local schools' sports is to sponsor an athletic team. Usually, the sponsor who picks up the tab gets the name of his or her business emblazoned on the athletes' jerseys and in any related printed material, such as sports banquet awards ceremony programs. That means every time your team takes the field or court, you get one free ad multiplied by the number of players who are colliding or dribbling.

# Gellin í with the Yellow Pages

It may not be sexy, but the Yellow Pages is still a great entry-level advertising medium for small business owners. When you have your business phone lines installed at your shop, you automatically will receive a line ad in the book. That is the small listing that gives the name of your shop, possibly your street address, and definitely your phone number. In addition, it is becoming increasingly common to find a business's Web site address in these line ads, although you will have to pay extra to make that happen. Regrettably, Yellow Pages will not divulge costs unless you are purchasing an ad, so contact a representative when you are ready to buy.

Of course, the real power of the Yellow Pages is not in the small type — it is in the larger ads, which are known as display ads. Such ads often are boxed, may have color elements and photographs, and certainly are the largest ads on the page. Presumably, these graphic elements draw attention to the ad, making it stand out among its peers.

But display ads are expensive. The cost depends on the city, the local distribution of the directory, and local market conditions. Generally, the more advertisers there are, the higher the cost will be. Here is an example: According to an article on Yellow Pages advertising in *Entrepreneur* magazine, a 1-inch display ad in a Manhattan, New York, directory costs $2,500, while a full-page ad would be $92,000. The same ads in a Manhattan, Kansas, directory would be $252 and $11,200, respectively. You can contact a Yellow Pages representative to determine the rate for your area, but as mentioned earlier, you are unlikely to get a rate quote unless you first agree to place the ad.

There are other drawbacks to display ads besides price. For example, if ads of a similar size for other detailers are on the same page you are, your ad may not be as much of an attention-getter as you would like. In addition, once you have signed a contract for a 12-month run of your ad, you are stuck paying the bill every month, even if you determine that your ad really is not garnering much business. One way to find out for sure whether your ad is working is to make it a regular practice to ask every customer where he or she heard about your business. If "Yellow Pages" is a top response, then you will know you are on to something.

But if you need a really good reason to consider that display ad, here it is: The "automobile detailing" category ranked No. 257 in the 2008 Yellow Pages Integrated Media Association (YPIMA) Top 300 Headings usage study. It is also important to note that you also can be in the online version of the big book, located at

**www.yellowpages.com**. The online version is searchable by city and state, type of business, or business name and will appeal to those who prefer cyber rather than print sources.

In case you are wondering how many people actually use the Yellow Pages, that 257th ranking equates to 5.7 million hits, according to YPIMA. In addition, another study by Knowledge Networks, called "The Y Advantage: Landscape 2008," indicated that nearly half (48 percent) of consumers still turn to the Yellow Pages for information. At 49 percent, search engines have surpassed the Yellow Pages as the most-used resource — but just barely.

# Other Print Resources

## Brochure basics

Another useful print resource for the start-up detailer is the brochure. Brochures can be configured in many different ways and in different sizes, but what they all have in common is enough space to sell the heck out of your business and the services you offer.

A brochure for a detailing shop consists of a service menu that describes all the services and packages it offers. It must have full contact information, preferably on both the front and back, and should have photos of beautifully detailed vehicles on the front and inside. You can fit all this information into what is known as a bi-fold brochure, which is an 8- by 9-inch sheet that has been folded to yield two panels that may be printed on both sides. Alternately, if you have a lot to say, you can create a tri-fold brochure, which is an 8 ½- by 11-inch sheet folded to create six panels (three on each side). Bi-fold and tri-fold brochures are specially sized to fit into the standard #10 business envelope, which comes in handy if you want to do a targeted mailing to people in your market area.

Print shops such as FedEx Office and AlphaGraphics, as well as office superstores such as OfficeMax, all can produce nice brochures on glossy stock for your shop. If you are doing business in an area that does not have a speedy print shop nearby, try an online printer instead. Online printers often have templates you drop your copy into so you can see right away what the final product will look like. Some also offer custom design services at higher prices. No matter which way you go, you will find that the cost of an Internet printer tends to be a little lower than a brick-and-mortar print shop. The only downside is that you do not have the luxury of seeing the brochure before it is printed — you simply have to wait until the brochure shows up in your mailbox. Nevertheless, using an online printer can be a cost-effective way to create brochures that really stand out. Prices vary, but expect to pay about $200 for 500 four-color tri-fold brochures.

In addition, Detailers Super Mall (Detail King's online store) sells a service menu program on CD that was created in Adobe® Illustrator and allows you to create a customized brochure that showcases the detailing services, packages, and products you offer. Because you will need both Illustrator and the knowledge to use it, you might have to find a graphic designer who can open this template-based program. It might be better just to have a designer create something new and exciting for you from scratch. But if you are interested in the CD, it sells for about $60. You can find information about it at **www.goestores.com/storename/detailking/dept/176158/ItemDetail-8587711.aspx**.

# CASE STUDY: MEASURE TWICE, CUT ONCE

### Create a Successful Business Brochure
### By Vann Baker

*Article reprinted with permission from Vann Baker of Design-First (**www. design-first.com**)*

Carpenters have a saying, "Measure twice, cut once," which is a good approach for saving expensive lumber and applies to creating a professional brochure for your company.

By clearly defining what your brochure should do and by doing some research first, your brochure can be effective and informative, and will get prospective clients' attention. By utilizing design and printing professionals and by paying close attention to details, you can have a brochure that truly represents your business and is something you can be proud to hand out and mail.

**Creating a great first impression**

A cover letter to a potential client can present only a small fraction of information about your business. Potential clients are often swamped with business mail, and a letter may be scanned for a couple of seconds, then trashed. A face-to-face meeting is a great way to tell a potential client about your business or expertise, but sometimes it is not possible to get a meeting with just a phone call or introductory letter. Or what if someone you met weeks ago suddenly becomes interested in your service — but cannot match your name with your business card in their Rolodex?

A brochure will fulfill all these business needs. Brochures are a great way to package a lot of information about yourself, your business, and your expertise into a format that is easily mailed or handed out at a business meeting or given to current clients to pass on to possible referrals.

**Brochure size**

Brochures range from a simple two-fold design using one sheet of 8.5- by 11-inch paper to an elaborate 9- by 12-inch pocket folder with eight pages stitched in and insert sheets.

Good brochure design involves not simply the creation of a flashy design, but a careful analysis of your target market, what level of sophistication is needed, and consideration of your market niche in order to make a great first impression.

And, last but certainly not least, your brochure should leave a potential client with something that he or she is hesitant to throw away.

Today, in the age of e-mail, multimedia presentations, and the Internet, it is easy to assume that a Web site can take the place of a printed brochure. Having a Web site cannot replace the immediate visual impact of placing a brochure into a prospective client's hands.

### Getting started

If you have never created a brochure, start by collecting a number of brochures (including competitors') that represent a wide range of quality — from simple one- and two-color brochures on textured stock, to slick, four-color glossy brochures.

By asking yourself what it is that makes a brochure attractive and effective to you, it will be easier to make a brochure for your own business that will convey the message and level of sophistication you require.

Next, you will need to create some basic brochure copy about your business. Even if you are not a professional writer, putting some thoughts and facts about your business down on paper will help make more concrete what information your brochure needs to convey.

When writing copy, ask yourself:

- Is my company an industry leader?
- Does my company have a market niche?
- What distinguishes my company from my competitor?
- Do we offer better value, service, or selection of products?
- Do we have anything new or different to promote?

Questions to ask yourself:

- Who is your target audience?
- What message will get a potential client's attention?
- What kinds of brochures and what level of sophistication are typically crossing your client's desk?

- What types of photographs or illustrations will help to convey your message?
- What format (e.g., self-mailer) should the brochure be in?

Key information to include in your brochure:

- Mailing address
- Phone number (and 800 number, if you have one)
- Fax number
- E-mail address
- Web site address

Be sure not to include in your brochure any information that is subject to change in the next 12 months or so. Also, be wary of using a specific person's name as a contact person unless he or she is someone you know is not going to leave in the next year. The same goes for printing photographs of people. There is no sense spending thousands of dollars to create a brochure, only to have it become outdated because someone leaves the company.

**What does it cost to produce a quality brochure?**

Brochure costs may range from a few hundred dollars to several thousand dollars. Because there are so many variables involved in producing a brochure, such as quality of paper, number of ink colors, use of photographs, number of brochures printed, and so on, it is difficult to estimate the final costs until all the specifications are determined.

Four-color process printing, varnishing, and special treatments such as die-cutting and foil-stamping can add additional costs to producing a brochure but may well be worth the cost if they enhance your brochure and the image you wish to project. Other cost considerations are whether you need professional photography, or help with writing or editing the copy for your brochure.

**Start with a realistic budget**

Even if you do not know all the details about your brochure when getting started, it is a good idea to create a basic budget.

Start with determining how many brochures you will need to use during the next 12 months, including those for mailings and sales meetings.

If you have seen a brochure with a similar amount of information and photographs as you need for your brochure, a designer can use it as a model for determining printing and production costs.

Another consideration when designing a brochure is postage. Larger brochures will be more expensive to mail, and if you are planning on doing a large mailing as part of your marketing, an oversized brochure may be expensive to mail.

Larger brochures do not fare well through the postal system, anyway; they often end up wrapped around other mail. Brochures that fit into a standard #10 business envelope give you the best buy in terms of postage and protection while mailing. Using a business envelope also allows you to include a cover letter and business card.

**Updating an existing brochure**

I worked with a client once who had sales of several million dollars a year but was still using a dated, unsophisticated brochure produced by a printer friend nearly ten years earlier. While reputation alone helped the company's sales, their outdated brochure was doing nothing to promote them as a cutting-edge, sophisticated company to potential customers who had never heard of them.

So if you have a brochure you produced a few years ago, it might be a good idea to have your brochure evaluated by a someone outside your company to make sure it projects the image of your company today and sets you apart from your competition. Often, a small company will produce an inexpensive brochure just to have something for a trade show or for telephone inquiries. While short-term needs are fulfilled, not having any kind of long-term plan for a package of coordinated materials will lead to a "hodge-podge."

As a business grows, the image of the business can outgrow the first brochure's image. Often, other collateral materials — such as pocket folders, product inserts, and so on — are produced at different times by different printers, and the result is a corporate image that is not coordinated, with different kinds of paper used and ink colors that do not match — in short, it is not professional at all.

It is tempting to take the "If it ain't broke, don't fix it" approach and leave an existing brochure alone — maybe for years. However, now could also be the ideal time to produce a truly professional brochure that will set you apart from your competition and give your potential clients something they will keep on their desk and will jog their memory when you do a follow-up call.

## Leverage both creativity and knowledge

Many businesses are producing promotional and sales materials internally or are relying on a printer to put a brochure together for them. There is nothing wrong with either of these approaches, provided you have the time and expertise to make all graphic design decisions that will produce a sophisticated brochure that is right on target.

It is rare to find a printer that has a graphic designer on staff who can put the right creative spark into your brochure design, and relying on in-house talent doesn't save you money when it actually costs you lost sales if the brochure is mediocre or poorly designed.

Using a graphic designer can free you from having to make all decisions about your brochure by yourself and will provide you with an outside perspective on how to communicate to your audience. A designer can provide you not only with typography experience, but can help you with selecting ink and paper. He or she also can give some direction with your brochure and help guide you through the process from start to finish.

In addition to making design decisions, a graphic designer can serve as your project manager and will see the brochure from concept through successful completion. Most designers work with several different printers and can provide you with a printer that has the capabilities to print your brochure. If you need help with writing your brochure copy, many designers can connect you with freelance writers and photographers who can help.

*Editor's note: Vann Baker is the president of Design-First and has been helping companies with branding and marketing for more than 25 years. Feel free to contact him at info@design-first.com or visit the Design-First Web site at **www.design-first.com**.*

## Postcards

Possibly the hardest-working advertising vehicle on the planet — next to your business card, that is — is the postcard, a cost-effective, unpretentious tool that provides plenty of space to convey a strong advertising message. What makes postcards especially useful is that they sail into customers' mailboxes as-is with no envelope required. Traditional wisdom holds that people are more likely to flip a postcard over and read the message, even if it is clearly advertising, than they are to rip open an envelope, unfold a sheet, and glance at it.

Detailers can use postcards to announce a grand opening, offer special deals, describe service packages, and keep the business top-of-mind for past customers who statistically are most likely to be the customers of the future. The two most common sizes are the 3 ½- by 5-inch and 4 ¼- by 6-inch cards. Both sizes mail for much less than the cost of a first-class letter — postage is 28 cents each, versus 44 cents each for a letter. This, of course, will save you a lot of money on your mailing. As with brochures, you can use a local print shop or an online printer to design and print your postcards. The cost is usually quite nominal. For example, one Internet printer found for this writing, Print Direct For Less (**www.printdirectforless.com**), charges $69 for 500 four-color postcards on glossy stock, or $182 for 5,000.

Of course, if you do decide to send out an advertising postcard, you will have to purchase a list of the names and addresses of consumers in your target area who might be detailing prospects. The Internet has many list brokers who can help you tailor a mailing list to meet your needs. The lists themselves can come to you either on pressure-sensitive mailing labels (labels that have adhesive on the back), or a disk that you can use to inkjet the names and addresses right onto the cards. If your budget is tight, use labels, which you and your family and friends can affix to postcards manually while watching a movie or a football game. If you decide you like the look of the ink-jetted addresses better, you will have to hire a mailing house to laser-print the postcards. One thing to remember about mailing lists, though, is that they are rented for one-time use. If you wish to use the list again for a subsequent mailing, you have to pay up again.

Another way to score a mailing list is to contact your local utility companies and even your state's division of motor vehicles. Both often rent their lists to businesses, sometimes at a very low cost. You will also want to start collecting the names, addresses, and e-mail addresses of your own customers as you acquire them so you can create your own personal mailing list. Capture that customer information by having every person who comes through the door fill out a "preferred customer" card that has spaces for name, address, phone number, and e-mail address. Just be sure you give your customers the opportunity to opt out of your mailings if they wish. The last thing you want to do is to start spamming your best customers, who definitely will have no trouble severing their ties with you if they perceive you to be an annoying spammer.

## Fliers

Another inexpensive advertising vehicle is the lowly flier. Often printed on affordable 20-pound paper in one color, fliers can be designed easily using a word processing program such as Microsoft® Word. Once printed, you can tuck them under windshield wipers, slip them under office doors, or leave them under doormats. But there are two caveats regarding flier distribution. First, make sure you have a permit to distribute the fliers. Check with your local municipality to learn the law and pay any necessary permit costs. Second, never put a flier in a mailbox. Mailboxes are considered federal property, so you can end up in a heap of trouble if someone complains that you are using his or her mailbox as an advertising drop-off point.

Fliers are the cheapest printed medium around. A quick-print shop can turn around 5,000 simple, 4- by 6-inch one-color fliers for about $20. Higher-quality fliers printed on glossy stock will cost about $100.

## Door hangers

These little advertising gems are remarkably inexpensive but can make quite an impact when left hanging from the front door of homes in your target market or from the doorknobs in high-rise office buildings.

The standard door hanger measures 4 ¼- by 11 inches and usually is printed on both sides on heavy paper stock or plastic. They have a die cut (a special cutout) that allows you to slip them over a doorknob or hang them from the rearview mirror of a freshly detailed vehicle. Unless you will be distributing the door hangers in a place with notoriously inclement weather, go for the paper stock rather than plastic because they are usually much less expensive to print.

At press time, one Internet printer, DoorHangers.com (**www. doorhangers.com**), was charging $300 for 10,000 door hangers printed on one side in two colors on nonglossy stock. That is an exceptional price that you may be able to duplicate simply by doing some Web surfing.

Once again, check to find out whether you need a permit to go door-to-door, gleefully dropping off door hangers. In addition, always speak to a commercial building's management office to verify that soliciting is permissible. But do not be surprised if you are turned down. In general, it is easier to get permission (i.e., a permit) to distribute in a residential neighborhood than a commercial building.

## Discount coupons

Everyone loves a bargain, and detailing customers are no different. So try offering coupons for a free service such as, say, a windshield wiper fluid top-off with every detail or a percent off certain services or packages you wish to promote. Giving a discount on the retail detailing products you carry also can be what is known in retail circles as a "loss leader," or a discounted product used to lure in customers in the hope they will make other purchases at the same time.

One really good place to distribute your car detailing coupons is at car shows or city cruises, where attendees are already primed to be in a car frame of mind. You also may find that the local auto dealership or auto-parts store may be willing to put a tidy little stack of your coupons on their service counters so customers can help themselves. Finally, consider using a "marriage mail" (shared mail) company such as ADVO (powered by Bagwell Marketing, **www.bagwell.com/advo-marriage-mail.html**) to distribute your coupons. With marriage mail, coupons and fliers from various companies are "ganged" together in a single envelope.

This reduces the distribution cost of the coupon while getting it into the hands of many potential customers in a target market in the most efficient way possible. Companies that specialize in marriage mail usually handle the design and printing of the coupons, making the process extremely simple. All you have to do is turn over some copy and pay for the completed product.

# Web Site

These days, everyone from the precocious preschooler down the street to your 90-year-old grandmother has a Web site — or a Facebook page, at the very least. But although it might seem that cyberspace is filling up fast, there definitely is room for your auto-detailing Web site. You absolutely must be out there promoting your business because your customers expect you to be. Savvy surfers are online 24/7 searching for services and products that fulfill their needs, and if you are not out there to greet them when they are looking for a detailer, they will find someone else.

A book of this length does not have enough space to discuss everything related to setting up a Web site. So here is a quick rundown on how to set up a site and launch it into cyberspace.

## Step 1: Write the Web site copy

This step often is enough to get people to forgo putting up a Web site altogether. But just because you are not a Hemingway in the making does not mean you cannot draft some appropriate Website copy. At the very least, make a list of what you wish to say on your Web site, from a welcome message on the home page to detailed descriptions of the services you will provide. Next, try to write a few paragraphs that crystallize your thoughts about those services. Finally, turn the copy over to an experienced freelance writer or copy editor, who can shape and mold it into polished and professional copy you can be proud of.

Among the information to include on your Web site is a service list with descriptions; a description of service packages; and a short business bio on the company and possibly yourself. You also can include a "library" of photos showing some of the gleaming, shiny vehicles you have detailed.

You probably can incorporate all this information in about three to four Web pages. On each page, include full contact information, including phone number, e-mail address, and Web address so customers do not have to go far to find it. Alternatively, you can include an e-mail return form that customers can fill out when requesting information. Place a link on your home page so customers just have to click once to be directed there.

To up the convenience quotient, set up your site to allow customers to book appointments online, or provide a shopping cart for making retail-product purchases online. Finally, you might want to include a blog or a detailing library with information or articles that might be of interest to customers, such as information about eco-friendly detailing products. If you want to use editorial material that has been published elsewhere, be sure to request permission in writing so you do not get into trouble later.

Incidentally, less is more when it comes to Web-site copy. People hate to keep scrolling down to read a message, so strive to keep it brief enough to fit on a single screen page. Obviously, you will not know how successful you have been at keeping the copy under control until you see it on the Web site, so at this point, try writing messages for each page that are no more than about 300 words. You can add to and expand them later if that is not enough copy.

## Step 2: Design the Web site

This is a task best left to the professionals, although if you have any experience with HTML and a lot of time, you could design your own site using a program such as Adobe® Dreamweaver CS4 software (**www.adobe.com**). But it is usually smarter to hire a professional Web designer, who for about $1,500 to $2,000 can create a fully functional Web site (one Web designer, **www.720Media.com**, will design a three-page Web site for as little as $500). Alternatively, if you wish to keep your costs down, consider hiring an information technology student or graduate from the local business school to create your site. Just be sure to ask to see some of the student's work to find out whether he or she has the experience to create the type of site you are looking for.

Of course, it is usually best to use an experienced Web professional to design your site. Whenever possible, select a designer who also is skilled at Web site maintenance and content management so you can put the entire job in the hands of just one capable computer professional.

## Step 3: Optimize the Web site

Once the Web site has been created, the next step is to optimize it in cyberspace by inserting keywords into the site language. Keywords are search words that lead people to your Web site when they use a search engine such as Google or Bing. For example, start by searching "detailing." On Bing, about 133 million hits will pop up, not all of which will be related to auto detailing. Next, try typing "auto detailing" into the browser, and you will see the field "narrow" to 24 million sites. Then type in "auto detailing Denver," and you will find yourself with just 1.03 million hits. Now, logically you know there could not possibly be 1.03 million detailers in a city with a metro-area population of approximately 2.5 million people. So some of those hits are occurring simply because the individual words (auto, detailing, and Denver) appear on a Web site somewhere — 1.03 million "somewheres." (Keep in mind these numbers do continually change, so you might find 27 million sites related to auto detailing when you do your own searching.)

Next, try "auto detailing metro Denver," and you will narrow the search results to 215,000. Now you are getting somewhere. Add "claying" to the mix, as in "auto detailing metro Denver claying," and you will get just 45 results. That is down from the 133 million you started with a few keystrokes ago and is much closer to the real number of businesses that actually offer claying as a detailing service in metro Denver.

The point is, any word that has any special significance to your business, from words that describe services to the names of products you use, must be inserted into your Web site so that when someone is searching for those terms, your Web site will be a "hit" for the surfer. This process of improving the quality of hits on a Web site is known as search engine optimization (SEO) and helps put your business at the forefront of search-engine searches. SEO also extends far beyond just keywords, to image searches, vertical searches, and more.

Here is why SEO is important. As you know, both from the Denver detailing example given above and your own Web surfing, Internet searches typically return an inordinate number of hits. These hits are usually displayed 10 to a page. Your primary goal should be to get your site to appear on the first page of the most popular search engines (Google, Bing, Yahoo!, Dogpile, and so on), because that will bring your site to the attention of the most people. Your second goal should be to get your site as high as possible on that first page. Choosing effective keywords is the first step in optimizing your Web site. Try brainstorming a list of keywords and phrases that apply to your business. Among the terms that might apply to a detailer are auto, car, detailing, auto detailing, car detailing, car cleaning, car washing and polishing, interior detailing, exterior detailing, and complete detailing. When using keyword phrases, keep them to no more than three to five words, and use very specific terms. Be sure to have a keyword phrase that includes the name of the market in which you are doing business, as in "detailing Walla Walla."

The sky is the limit on the number of keywords you can use. If you plan to include special services in your service menu, such as paintless dent repair or window tinting, include those terms in your keyword list as well. Obviously, not every keyword will appear on every page, so work with your Web consultant to decide which words and phrases are most relevant on each page and concentrate on those.

Another way to improve SEO on your site is to update the content on a regular basis, as search engines tend to favor sites that have new content. This is a good reason to start a blog — every new entry gives you that little added advantage of being seen as a fresh, new site in the "eyes" of a search engine.

Obviously, there is more to SEO than this, and this is probably more than you signed up for when you decided to start a detailing business. Your content manager can help you optimize your site and confer with you on other techniques to improve your search-engine ranking.

## Step 4: Select a domain name

Another important step in the SEO process is the selection of a domain name. The domain name is your Web site's address, or URL. Commonly, auto detailers name their businesses after themselves, as in Kenneth Russell Detailing, which means the name would translate into a URL of kennethrusselldetailing.com on the Internet. If the .com URL is not available, you could try to get the name with an extension of .net, .us, .info, or one of several other extensions.

When you are ready to select your domain name, go to a name provider such as **www.GoDaddy.com**, where you can type in your chosen name and see whether it is available. As with your DBA, have a couple of names in reserve just in case your first choice is taken. Take kennethrusselldetailing.com, for instance. If that name has been claimed, you could try RussellDetailing.com, KRDetailing.com, DetailingByKen.com, and so on, then move on to trying the other extensions listed above if those second- and third-string names are already active, too. Another strategy, if you really like the name you have selected, is to try the same name with a different ending, as in .net or .us. Be aware, however, that some search engines favor .com endings over others, so you might be better off simply selecting a different name.

Domain names are registered in one-year increments for about $10 per year. Search "domain names" in a search engine and you will get many companies to choose from.

Incidentally, some Web developers prefer that you secure the domain name and hosting first before writing copy. That makes it easier to set up the site instead of having to migrate it somewhere else later. Discuss this with your Web developer to be sure.

## Step 5: Find a Web hosting service

A Web host provides the server space and connectivity your Web site requires to operate in cyberspace. As with domain name providers, you can choose from among many Web hosts, many of which provide free domain-name registration. So shop around before you commit. According to the Web Hosting Choice Web site (**www.webhostingchoice.com**), the top 10 Web hosts as of this writing are:

1.  **www.JustHost.com**

2.  **www.Webhostingpad.com**

3.  **www.DreamHost.com**

4.  **www.HostMonster.com**

5.  **www.BlueHost.com**

6.  **www.InMotionHosting.com,**

7. **www.HostClear.com**

8. **www.HostGator.com**

9. **www.GoDaddy.com**

10. **www.Yahoo.com**

## Step 6: Keep it updated

Once the Web site is up and running, it is essential to keep it updated and current, or else it becomes nothing more than a boring place marker in space. In particular, you will want to post information about shop specials and discounts that will help increase business. For this reason, ask your content manager to create a Web site template that you easily can update yourself. If you do not have the time or desire to be your own Web editor, your content manager can do it for you.

SEO experts recommend refreshing your content at least once a week. If that is not possible, try to do it at least once a month. Refreshes can include adding articles, a banner announcing a detailing special, new photos of recently detailed vehicles, or blog posts.

Other cyber tools can complement your Web site activities nicely, including Facebook, Twitter, and blogs. *These options are discussed in Chapter 11, which touches on publicity techniques you can use to promote your business.*

# Other Advertising Vehicles

Besides the Yellow Pages, traditional printed materials, and your Web site, here are a few other advertising tools to try:

**Point-of-purchase (POP) materials:** As the name implies, these advertising materials are placed at, near, or around the cash register or sales counter as a way to promote a particular item, brand, or service, especially those that are new. POP materials can include posters, countertop displays, shelf signs, and even vinyl floor graphics, and their purpose is the same: to spur new sales. Business.com (**www.business.com**) has a directory of companies that sell POP materials and displays. Some companies to check out include Influence Communications (**www.influenceme.com**), Britten Banners (**www.brittenbanners.com**), and Full Steam (**www.fullsteam.com**).

**Trinkets and trash:** For years, marketers have rather irreverently referred to advertising specialty items imprinted with a company's name, logo, and contact information as "trinkets and trash." But these items are hardly trash when they make it into the pockets or purses of current and prospective customers who will be reminded of your detailing shop every time they see or use the item. You can pick from scores of advertising specialties, from pens and water bottles, to automotive-themed items such as key chains, car fresheners, license-plate frames, sunshades, and travel mugs. Because the main point of distributing such items is to increase awareness of your business, pick items that people use all the time, such as pens or pocket planners, and start distributing them to every customer who crosses the threshold, as well as every other person you meet wherever you go (including the chamber of commerce, grocery store, post office, church, and so on). You will be surprised at how fast the buzz for your business will build just by distributing some 50-cent specialty items.

**On-hold messages:** It is such a simple idea: Play a recorded advertising message while people are on hold to induce them to make additional purchases. The technique works well because you have a captive audience, so craft the best, most irresistible message possible to tempt callers to use your services. Many companies online can help you empower your phone to be a dynamic sales machine. Search "on hold messages" to get started, or try **www.marketingmessages.com**, **www.easyonhold.com**, or **www.onholdmarketing.com**.

**Business cards:** The humble business card is actually one of the most powerful and inexpensive sales tools you have. Like the advertising specialties mentioned above, you can distribute them far and wide. Make arrangements to leave a supply in a small stand (available at the office superstores) on the counter of automotive-related businesses with whom you have a reciprocal advertising agreement. For example, you could work out a deal with a local car wash to have your business included in any advertising the car wash does. Include your business card in any mailings you send out, including invoices sent to your corporate or fleet customers-to-be. Business cards are very inexpensive to print: about $30 for 1,000 cards in a standard layout from an office superstore. There is no design work necessary: The office stores have a variety of templates to select from and can include logos or four-color art for a nominal fee, so there is no reason to buy one of those do-it-yourself kits for printing cards on your home computer. The sole exception might be if you are running out of printed cards just before a critical networking or car event, but otherwise, do not go there. You are a professional, so even something as small as a business card should reflect that.

These are by no means the only advertising tools at your disposal. For example, you also could buy space on the cable TV local-access channel. Or, you can advertise on a local radio station (during drive time, of course). Broadcast media, however, tend to be pricey, perhaps too much so for your start-up budget. Nevertheless, keep them in the back of your mind for later down the road when you are making more money and can afford such "big ticket" advertising venues.

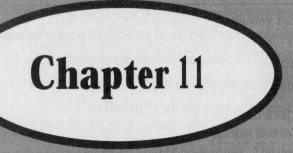

## Chapter 11

## Publicity 101 for Fun and Profit

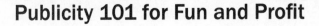

The last chapter was all about the various advertising strategies you can employ to increase awareness of your business and promote your services. This chapter covers the tools you can use to get free or low-cost publicity that will be just as valuable as any advertising you pay for.

Some advertising and marketing experts believe that companies should not spend money on advertising until they have established their presence in the marketplace and their brand identity. To a cash-strapped entrepreneur, that might sound like a really good idea. But the reality is, it is best to do both; namely, to create carefully planned advertising materials and place them in the media with the greatest potential for return — and to whip up some carefully planned publicity materials and hope they get into print or on the air.

Yes, you read that right. You hope your efforts will be recognized. Because unlike advertising, which is a sure thing because you paid for it, publicity efforts do not always reap immediate bene-fits. But when they do, they can give your business a tremendous boost, which is why it is important to start promoting yourself right away. Here is a rundown on some simple things you can do to score some of that high-visibility publicity.

# Newsletters

Newsletters are effective vehicles for keeping in touch with cus-tomers and your services and products. After you make the initial investment in Microsoft® Office or another software program that has newsletter templates, your cost to produce a newsletter will be quite low. If you e-mail it, your cost will go down even more. Almost anything can go in a newsletter, but some good topics to cover for a detailing-shop newsletter include:

- Description of services (to tempt readers to book them)

- Information about vehicle care packages you offer

- Stories about weather-related or seasonal car-care issues

- Reviews of the detailing products you sell and a descrip-tion of how to use them

- Information about car clinics you speak at or hold at the shop

- News about local automotive activities, such as city cruises or hot-rod meets

- Details about participation in charitable events

- Testimonials from satisfied customers

- Details about your customer referral program (i.e., refer a customer, get a discount)

- Newsletter subscriber-only coupons and specials, which will help build your mailing list faster

## General newsletter guidelines

Newsletters do not have to be lengthy. An 8 ½- by 11-inch, one-page newsletter printed on two sides is great for a detailing shop because it gives you just enough space to get enthusiastic about your services and detailing packages but does not cause "too much information syndrome" in readers. In fact, feel free to fill only one side of the newsletter, if that is all the news you have. Leave space on the bottom third of the reverse side of the newsletter so you can affix a mailing label there rather than going through the trouble and expense of stuffing the newsletters into envelopes before mailing. And here is a tip: One-sided newsletters can be repurposed as fliers if the layout is simple enough — just be sure to take off the date before you reprint them.

To keep the cost down, write the newsletter yourself or have your shop manager do the deed. If you are really strapped for time or if writing is just not your thing, hire a freelance writer to help. Nothing says "amateur" more than a newsletter that is poorly written or filled with misspellings or sloppy typos.

Publish your newsletters on a regular schedule, even if there is a big gap between issues (such as publishing in the spring and fall). If they are hit-or-miss, or if they come out erratically, it may appear that the newsletter is an afterthought rather than something the customer will find useful. So establish a regular schedule — say, quarterly or three times a year — and stick with it. If you do not have enough news to fill an issue, make a coupon the issue's centerpiece and send it out. To make the issue seem timely, always include some seasonal material, such as stories on how to winterize a car or how to minimize the effect of the summer sun on a vehicle's finish.

Because you will not have your own client mailing list when you start your business, you will have to buy a mailing list. *Review Chapter 10 for more details on obtaining a list.* Remember that you are allowed to use a mailing list only once, and you will have to pay for it again each time you use it. Eventually, as you build a stable of clients and exchange cards with other business owners you meet, you can start compiling your own mailing list rather than using purchased lists.

Finally, because you should treat newsletters as an important part of your marketing strategy, build a newsletter archive on your Web site so customers can refer to past issues for tips and information. This is an easy way to drive customers to your Web site and remind them what you can do for them.

## E-mail newsletter guidelines

Although an e-mail newsletter is much cheaper to produce and easier to deliver than a print newsletter, do not make one until you have a Web site up and running. The reason is logistical: E-mail newsletters usually do not contain full-blown articles. Rather, they contain brief introductions to each story that are about a paragraph long, accompanied by links to the articles. Although those links should transport readers to your Web site, they should not take them to your home page. You do not want to make people work too hard to find the information you promised them in the newsletter. They may just click through to the next Web site if they discover they have not been directed right to the information they were expecting. Here is another tip: Try to use short URLs as clickable article links and place them on a line of their own, rather than using a lengthy URL like this: **www.marketingcharts. com/topics/directories/yellow-pages-search-engines-tops-for-business-search-7199/?utm_campaign=newsletter&utm_source=mc&utm_medium=textlink**.

Such long URLs usually break poorly and do not look very attractive on the page, while short ones stand out among the copy, visible on the screen at any given time.

If you do not have a Web site yet, all is not lost. Just create a one-page PDF (portable document format) newsletter that you can paste into or attach to an e-mail. Of course, not everyone is willing to open attachments, so all your hard work might end up being for nothing.

When sending your newsletter, treat the subject line as a headline for some of the content in the newsletter. For example, "Dent repair makes cars look like new again" is much more evocative than "Bo's Detailing Newsletter." Just keep the length of the line to no more than 60 characters so it does not spill over into a second line.

# News Releases

A news release (press release) is a promotional article of no longer than two pages (and preferably less) that focuses on positive news about a business. Car detailers typically do not send out releases, usually because they simply do not have a lot of news to pass along to the media. There are times, however, when you should let the world know about your activities, for both public relations and goodwill value:

- Buzz about your grand opening (a local paper might be especially interested in this)

- Charitable activities you are involved in, including contributions you make to local organizations or sponsorships of high school sports teams

- Workshops you are teaching on the art of detailing

News releases need to be short and pithy because the people who receive them may have time only to glance at them. As a result, it is important to have a catchy headline and attention-grabbing first line on your release. But no matter how interesting the release is, you should know that sending it to a news outlet does not guarantee that it will appear in print. A lot of times, however, local newspapers or magazines simply have a hole to fill, so they suddenly become very interested in your information, and voilà! — you find yourself in the newspaper. There is no charge for that, either. The same thing happens with broadcast news, although in that case, a writer or producer from a TV, cable, or radio station might call and request an interview for an on-air story. Then, at last, you will get your 15 minutes of fame. *The standard format for a printed news release can be found on the companion CD-ROM.*

To make the job even easier, use one of the free press release templates on the Microsoft® Office Web site at **http://office.microsoft.com/en-us/templates/default.aspx**.

Now, because this is the 21$^{st}$ century, editors these days generally prefer to receive their news by e-mail. *A sample format e-mailed news release is included in the companion CD-ROM.*

Add a recipient's name and an attention-getting subject line and send it on its way. Do not just attach the release. Editors at most news outlets are cautious about opening attachments, so if you send an e-mail just with an attachment and nothing in the body, you can say sayonara to your release — it will be deleted in a flash.

## Writing the release

You do not have to be a public relations professional or a journalist to write a news release, as long as you keep your writing simple and apply the journalists' "Five Ws (and One H)" rule. That stands for, "who, what, where, when, why, and how." Here is how that would work when gathering information for a release for a detailing shop's grand opening celebration:

- **Who:** Kenneth Russell Detailing
- **What:** Grand opening celebration
- **When:** Saturday, Sept. 28
- **Where:** 27249 Lawrence St.
- **Why:** To introduce the public to the best detailing services in the Detroit metro area
- **How:** Detailing demonstrations continually from 10 a.m. to 4 p.m.

Then it is just a matter of writing a few sentences about each point to give the reader enough information about the topic to be able to act. And remember: Less is more. You do not need to spend a lot of time developing an award-winning release when a "down-and-dirty" release that gives just the facts will do the job just as well.

If this sounds like way too much trouble for someone committed to car excellence rather than words, or if your grammar and punctuation skills are not up to the challenge, you always can hire a freelance writer to do the deed for you. Your business contacts and friends undoubtedly will be able to give you a lead.

## Creating a mailing list

Editors today tend to prefer receiving e-mailed releases. But no matter whether you are planning to send your release via e-mail or snail mail, you will need a list of current editors to send the release to. Look up contact information online for each newspaper or broadcast company, or call for the names and addresses you cannot find online. If your metro area has a lot of media outlets, you will find it more efficient to use a media directory to look up contact information. One such directory is Mondo Times (**www.mondotimes.com**), which covers media literally from around the world. There is no cost to use Mondo Times. Another directory, the Finder Binder (**www.finderbinder.com**), covers the media in some of the country's largest markets more extensively than Mondo Times. Contact Finder Binder directly for the price of the directory in your market.

No matter how you compile the list, always find out the name of the editor who should receive the release and address it to that person. There is no point in sending a time-sensitive news release to a general box because there is no telling when (and if) someone will get around to opening the mail or reading the e-mail messages.

# Networking

If you have ever been to a speed-dating event or attended a job fair, you already know the power of networking. It works for service businesses such as detailing, too. By getting to know other business owners at venues such as roundtables, meet-and-greet events, or even church socials, you can create a demand for your services. Granted, it might not happen overnight, but the more business cards and handshakes you distribute, the more likely it is that someone will stop by for detailing services or will refer you to their colleagues.

Also, business networking events are wonderful forums for bartering services. For instance, say you meet the owner of an office-cleaning company at a business forum. There may come a time when your employees cannot take care of the waiting room and restrooms in your shop and detail cars, too. So you unearth the business card of the cleaning company owner, call or make an appointment, and offer to trade detailing for cleaning. If one service is more costly than the other, you can make up the difference in cash. In the meantime, you get a service you need at a reduced price because you will be providing the other owner with a service in return.

All you need to network effectively is a stack of business cards, a winning smile, and a membership in a couple of professional organizations. It also helps to get involved personally in some of the organization's activities or committees as a way to make your presence known and spread your reputation.

# Public Speaking

According to a 2008 story on **www.DiscoveryHealth.com**, people are less afraid of going to hell, contracting cancer, or being swept away by a tornado than they are of public speaking. So you might think it is an insane idea even to consider putting yourself through such agony just to promote your business. But meeting the public and discussing what you do during an informal presentation is a great and logical way to position yourself as a detailing expert, which in turn helps convince the public that you are the person to contact for every detailing service they need.

You might be surprised by how many opportunities you can find to wax poetic about your profession. Start with car-care clinics. Hold one at your shop or offer to present one at the meeting of a local car club. If your community has a summer car cruise, rent a space along the cruise route and talk to people who attend the event. You also will find that business organizations, libraries, garden clubs, and even benevolent organizations are always looking for speakers to fill a hole in a program. All it takes are a few phone calls to line something up. You also might be able to teach a one-time class or seminar on auto detailing at a local community college. This has an additional benefit: You could meet a couple of students from the audience who might make good employees.

Now, public-speaking anxiety is one thing, but you probably are also wondering why on earth you would share information about your detailing techniques and secrets with nonpaying audiences.

The reason is simple: They may have the desire, but not everyone in attendance will have the time or the skills to detail his or her own vehicle. Or, having heard what hard work detailing entails, some may decide they would rather pay someone else to do it. Both scenarios can yield new business for your shop, as well as word-of-mouth referrals.

For this reason, always carry a supply of business cards with you to such events. But do not break them out until you are asked for one. A business meeting or class is not the place for blatant self-promotion, but you certainly can produce a card if someone asks for it.

# Fundraisers

Fundraisers are another no-cost way to get the word out about your shop and position yourself as a caring community leader. Whenever someone comes to you with a request for detailing services that can be auctioned off or offered as a prize in a drawing to benefit a nonprofit or other worthy organization, always agree. The organization will be grateful, and you will gain valuable exposure for your business among those who attend the event. Best of all, you will not pay anything for this exposure beyond the cost of the prize you donate. You simply do what you do best (detail cars) in exchange for the promotional opportunity.

# Viral Promotion

No discussion of free promotion would be complete without touching on Facebook and Twitter, the two social networking sites that have revolutionized the world of Internet information.

Both are increasingly becoming the tools of choice for promoting a business and networking with other business professionals. Plus, they are both free.

## Facebook

Facebook (**www.facebook.com**) is useful for small-business owners because it allows you to create a profile page about yourself, as well as a separate page about your business. Once you have set up the key information on your business page discussing who you are and what you do, you can add other content, including pictures and descriptions of your services. Then you let the people who are interested in your services know they can find you on Facebook. One way to do this is to create a link to Facebook on your Web site to direct surfers there; another is to put the Facebook logo on your business cards and other collateral materials, and your Facebook URL in your e-mail signature.

This might sound redundant. After all, your Web site already has all this promotional stuff on it. But look at it this way: Facebook is just one more promotional tool you will have in your Internet toolbox. The only thing you might consider paying for is an ad on Facebook because it can get more exposure for your page. But you can reap the benefits of Facebook without spending a penny, which is reason enough to take advantage of all the advertising opportunities it offers.

Here are some easy ways you can gain free exposure for your business using Facebook:

- Post news about your business on your wall through your status updates. Those updates might include changes in service hours, changes in personnel, charitable contributions, and more. If it is newsworthy, it can go on the wall.

- Provide links to useful articles about detailing, weather conditions that can play a factor in a car's finish, and anything else that might be of interest to car mavens. You do not have to worry that this will give people too much information and drive them to detail their own rides. The hope is that this will entice them to drive to your shop with cash or credit cards in hand.

- Use the "find friends" feature as a way to expand your network and search for mutual friends on your contact list. It is a great way to open the door to future business.

- Start a group page. Try, say, establishing a detailing group for car aficionados, which might attract car buffs while reminding them at every turn that you are a "buffing master."

Include your photo and enough information about yourself so visitors can put a face to the name when they visit your page. People like to know the person they are doing business with, so use your Facebook page to tell readers a little about yourself in a friendly, inviting manner.

Of course, while these techniques are quite helpful, you still have to optimize your Facebook page so it floats to the top — or as close to the top as possible — of the Internet universe. The way to do that is though search engine optimization, or SEO. Basically what that means is finding ways to make your page show up higher in a Google keyword search. One way to do that is to use your "about" box as the depository for as much keyword-filled text as possible. There is a 250-word limit, but if you choose words wisely, you can really amp up the keyword quotient.

If this all sounds like Greek to you, do not despair. There are now social networking consultants who can guide you through the SEO process. For that matter, you probably could ask just about any college student for help. But for now, the most important thing is to head over the Facebook, sign up for a free account, and explore the possibilities. When you are ready to rock your page, ask for help.

## Twitter

Then there is Twitter (**www.twitter.com**), a micro-blogging system that small-business owners can use to keep in touch with customers and form a professional development network.

Twitter users send messages of 140 characters or less, called "tweets," to their followers, who are people who choose to join their network. You also can send photos and audio clips. So let us say business is slow and you would like to get in a few more jobs before calling it a day. You could send a tweet to your network that says, "15 percent off interior detailing for the first two callers to 800-555-6789! Offer ends at 6 p.m."

Like Facebook, Twitter has a whole cyber hierarchy behind it that can be manipulated to increase the number of followers you have. One simply way to increase your Twitter presence is to use hashtags. A hashtag is a word or term that has a hash mark (#) in front of it, like, for instance, #cardetailing. When you use a hashtag, you are tagging the post for that specific word so it can be tracked and posted in real time on the Twitter hashtags site. Then, all you do is go to the site and click on that particular word to see all the posts that have been tagged. It is like a shortcut to the hot news related to virtually any subject, or kind of like Twitter SEO. You do have to opt into the hashtags site to be able to follow it; it is just a matter of visiting the site and signing up for free.

Another way to spark some interest in your business is by using trending topics, another free Twitter service. Trending topics are basically are extremely short exchanges of information (tweets) on whatever is happening at the moment. Just sign up at **http:// twitter.com/trendingtopics** to join the fun of talking about any-thing that is on your mind at any given time.

Finally, you can even use Twitter to build your brand. Become a follower of business giants and detailing experts, then learn from their comments. The tweets are often off-the-cuff and unguarded, so you might pick up information you can use to improve your own brand. You also can use Twitter to keep an eye on your per-sonal or professional reputation.  Just go to **http://search.twitter. com** and enter your brand name to see what people are saying about you. If the information is good, then you are in. If it is not, then you have a chance to make things right.

Clearly, there is way more to both Twitter and Facebook than can be covered in a book of this length that is intended to be a guide for building a car detailing business. For more information, con-tact one of those social networking consultants mentioned earlier, talk to other social networking users, or pick up one of the many books now available on the subject. It is a whole new world out there — and you can and should be part of it.

# Blogs

Before Facebook and Twitter, there were weblogs, or blogs. Blogs are personal, online entry-style sites usually attached to company Web sites that are mostly unconstrained in terms of length (like Twitter) or content. Written in reverse chronological order, blogs contain commentary, opinions, insight, news articles, and other content. It is usually the blogger's intention to create a following for his or her words of wisdom, which means they have to be scintillating, riveting, and pertinent, or else the blogger will be met with dead air and few readers.

Business owners use blogs as a way to drive traffic to their Web sites and hopefully stimulate sales. A detailing blog on your Web site would be a great place to promote and build excitement for your services and products. You can use your blog as an online newsletter or as a forum to comment on issues of interest to the detailing community and consumers alike. However, it is not enough to occasionally dump content into a blog. If you truly want to use a blog as an advertising and marketing tool, you have to post regularly, and the content has to be created to interest readers and not be just slapped together. Some small-business owners even hire freelance writers to write their blog posts so that readers who return for more are not disappointed by the static content. It is worth noting that there are now more than 100 million blogs on the Internet, which may dampen your enthusiasm for the forum somewhat. But considering that blogs are yet another overdone way to drum up free publicity, it might be worth your while to do one.

You can blog about anything that strikes your fancy. Say, for instance, you just attended a manufacturer's seminar demonstrating a new piece of power equipment. Tell the world about it through a blog post. Or maybe you heard a tasty bit of information at an auto show about the vehicles of the future. Share that, and speculate about how detailers will evolve to handle any future challenges. You also can discuss articles you have read that are thought provoking, or simply vent about an issue that is driving you crazy, like maybe how postal rates keep going up and making your detailing products more expensive. As long as the commentary is interesting, it is appropriate for your blog.

A blog is also a great place to post links to other information, pictures of vehicles you have detailed, or videos of yourself in action. Do not worry about giving away the store by showing your brilliant detailing techniques. The fact is, many people may have the desire to do their own detailing, but not the time or patience. So you actually might inspire some would-be weekend warriors to pick up the phone or e-mail you for an appointment.

No matter what you do, you should have an RSS feed on your Web site. This allows you to deliver updated Web content to your subscribers — those who ask to be fed such information automatically — as fast as possible. It can be a good way to promote services, sell products, and otherwise inform your followers about what is new and exciting at your shop. List your RSS feed on the major news feeds (including **www.Syndic8.com** and **www. NewsIsFree.com**) and you will extend your reach even faster.

As with the other social networking opportunities mentioned here, your blog will benefit from SEO so it appears high in a Google keyword search. Your Web developer or social networking consultant can help with that, too.

# Grand Opening Celebration

Out of all the promotional techniques discussed in this chapter, a grand opening celebration will cost the most, but it also can make the biggest splash in terms of impact and visibility. The good news is you can pull off an interesting and exciting grand opening to introduce yourself and your services to the community without spending a fortune. Just lay out a few refreshments (coffee, soft drinks, hot dogs, and cookies would suffice), have some promotional items on hand, and you are all set to welcome your public. The bad news is it really only works if you have a brick-and-mortar facility; home-based detailers and mobile detailers will need to try other promotional strategies instead.

Because so many weekend warriors like to buff and polish their rides on the weekend, you should schedule your event on a weekend. Choose a date that does not coincide with a national holiday or a time when families traditionally travel, such as the last week of August right before schools starts, the week between Christmas and New Year's Day, or the local college or high school spring break. By that same token, a spring or summer grand opening is usually best because the weather is optimal. If you are launching your business in January, you will just have to hope the weather will not be dreary on open-house day.

Furthermore, schedule the event for a few weeks after you actually start detailing. Before you invite the public in for a look, it is important to make sure things are running smoothly and the staff, members if any, are working harmoniously. Test all the detailing equipment and actually detail it so it shines. You also should have the shop cleaned and polished so it rivals the luster on the vehicles you detail. Select a starting time for the event that mirrors your regular shop hours, although do not worry — if you normally work a ten- to 12-hour day, you do not have to entertain your adoring public for that long. About four to six hours is just right, depending on whether you have help (employees) to assist.

The centerpiece of your grand opening should be hands-on detailing demonstrations. If possible, arrange the shop so you have a staging area, and place rented chairs in front of it in rows so you can accommodate a large number of people. If that will not work in your space, then park the vehicle to be detailed in the center of the area you choose and allow people to crowd around it. During the warmer months, you also could hold the event in your parking lot if it has sufficient room for both detailing demonstrations and parking for guests, but make sure it will be easy to move everything inside if the weather deteriorates. Also make sure you have a few people standing by to answer questions during the demonstrations. To keep your visitors happy, offer refreshments. Soft drinks, simple munchies such as pretzels and small wrapped candies, hot dogs, and even pizza bites can be good choices. Balloons and face painting for the kids will help turn the event into a family-friendly day of fun.

Also, be sure to have an assortment of advertising specialties such as imprinted pens and key chains on hand. *Refer to Chapter*

*10 for more information on how to feature these items.* Consider having a drawing for a free exterior detailing or a basket of detailing products. The point of having a drawing is to collect names for your first mailing list, so make sure the entry form asks for full contact information, including an e-mail address, and has a check-off box requesting permission to send advertising messages to the entrant via regular mail or e-mail. Put a stack of business cards and detailing-service brochures near the bowl where you will collect entries.

Send out a press release announcing the event, but do not stop there. Make a few phone calls to invite key members of the local media personally. Although there are no guarantees, a two-minute call can increase the chances that you will get some media coverage and successfully jump-start your promotional efforts. You also might invite key elected officials as a way to kick off your run as a new community and civic supporter on the right wheel.

## Chapter 12

**Financing Primer**

O ne of the factors that makes a car detailing business so attractive to fledgling small-business owners is that you can
start it on a shoestring budget. Despite this, even the most frugal
one-person business owner will need more than just a bucket and
some car polish to run a detailing business successfully — and
possibly also some financing to keep the business going during
the lean early years. This chapter covers the various back-office
costs you are likely to encounter in the start-up phase, from operational expenses to human resources costs, followed by a look
at how to obtain any necessary financing.

# Typical Operational Costs

As you will recall from Chapter 6, you can sink *a lot* of cash into
detailing equipment, tools, and supplies — or you can start making money using just the basics. Because it is possible to do a
bang-up job detailing cars using just those basics, that definitely

is the way you should go. Low start-up costs really do equate to greater business success because you are not starting out with a gigantic financial liability that can drag you down — and maybe even bankrupt you — when business is slow.

The same thing goes for recurring overhead costs. Keep them modest and you automatically increase your chances of success, even in a slow market or during months of inclement weather. The expenses discussed here are considered essential for car detailing operations, but you certainly can pick and choose which ones are absolutely necessary at this point in your business cycle.

*To help you visualize the types of expenses and income you can expect to encounter as a new detailing-business owner, you can find a sample income statement in the companion CD-ROM.* The basic template for this statement, which was adapted for use by a detailing business, comes from the Microsoft® Office Web site (**http://office.microsoft.com**). Use the search term "income statement 1 year" to go to the same Excel template, which you then can download and customize for your own use. QuickBooks also has templates you can customize. The next few sections will discuss the most common monthly operational costs for a car detailer.

## Mortgage/rent payment

Right off the bat, this is an expense you can avoid if you are a one-person business owner — and in fact, it is one you *should* avoid as long as possible. Set up shop in your own garage, pole barn, or covered breezeway — assuming your community or landlord will allow this — and you will be able to avoid a mortgage or rent payment, perhaps indefinitely. Because mortgage and rent costs do eat up a considerable amount of cash each month, using space you already own or rent is always preferable.

Clearly, if you will be running a larger operation — say, with several employees and two to three bays — you will need to buy or lease a facility. You will incur the greatest cost if you purchase or lease a standalone building. Unfortunately, it is difficult to estimate exactly how much such a mortgage or lease might cost because each metropolitan market differs. A recent Grubb & Ellis Industrial Trends Report, which tracked conditions in 58 metropolitan areas, indicated that the average asking lease rate for industrial space was $5.54 per square foot. Figure out how much space you will need and do the math to estimate your monthly lease cost. Do keep in mind, however, that leasing rates have declined significantly in recent years because of the economic downturn, so they are likely to rise again just as soon as the economy recovers. Negotiate your lease agreement carefully to lock in low rates for as long as possible.

If you would like a real-time estimate of lease costs in your community, check out **www.leasemls.com**. Enter in your location, the type of property you are seeking (try "industrial" for a detailing shop), the building type (specify automotive-related here), the amount of space you are seeking, and the rate you wish to pay, and you will get a list of available buildings that meet your requirements. Naturally, the amount you wish to pay and the amount a lease actually costs in your community may differ significantly, so call a commercial real estate broker for help, as he or she can provide information about market conditions and steer you in the right direction.

Another option is to lease space in an auto mall. Auto malls generally consist of a group of related automotive-service providers — dealerships, auto-glass repair shops, tire stores, and so on — under one roof or situated in close proximity to each other. If the businesses are all under a single roof, so much the better — the cost to lease probably will be lower.

A final option is to form a business relationship with an auto dealership (if you intend to go after that segment of the detailing market) or a car wash that does not already offer detailing services. Essentially, you would be subletting space from the dealership or car wash to ply your trade — and getting a built-in clientele, to boot.

Again, it is difficult to estimate a cost for auto-mall space or space leased from another business because the rate depends both on the landlord's whim and what the local leasing market will bear. A commercial real estate broker may be able to steer you to an interested landlord, or you can try calling a business's facilities manager directly to inquire about availability and negotiate a rate.

If you are planning to offer mobile services, you have one more worksite option: You can provide services right in the parking lot of commercial office buildings or other public spots. Naturally, you cannot simply show up in the parking lot on a bright, sunny morning, spread out your water-reclamation equipment, and start detailing. You definitely must obtain permission from the building owner, who may or may not charge you for the privilege. Even so, it is reasonable to assume that any such rental fee will be fairly nominal, as you will be using only a couple of parking spaces in the lot. It is possible, however, that the owner might want a per-vehicle fee.

For the purposes of this book, it is assumed that you initially will work on your own property.

## Utilities

You must include in your monthly expense statement the cost of the electricity, gas, and water you use to run your detailing business. If you are leasing space, your landlord may include some or all of these costs in your monthly payment; otherwise, you are on your own. If you are working out of a facility on your own property, you need to calculate the cost of the utilities used to maintain your household versus the cost incurred by the business. The easiest way to do this is to refer to pre-business utility bills and estimate what percentage of the bill can be attributed to business use. For example, let us say that your new Car Detailing Emporium, which you set up in your garage, constitutes 20 percent of the square footage of your home and garage combined. Multiply the utility costs on previous bills by 20 percent to arrive at a figure that you can attribute to the business. To get the most accurate figure, average the utility costs over the previous 12 months, then divide that figure by the percentage you determined.

## Personnel

For some small-business owners, adding employees to the payroll is a tangible sign of success. After all, if you expect to have so much work that you will need help to handle it, you must be poised for instant business success, right?

Maybe, maybe not. The reality is that an overstaffed small business can quickly find itself deep in red ink. To put it bluntly, employees are expensive, both in terms of how much you must pay them and Uncle Sam for their services, and how much time you must spend managing them. This is not to say you should not hire helpers for your business if you truly need them. But give the matter a lot of thought and, if at all possible, start off as a lone ranger until you can gauge how successful your business will be. If hiring employees is unavoidable at this stage of your business development, here is what you can expect to pay:

**Hourly wage:** The current federal minimum wage is $7.25 per hour. Therefore, a part-time worker who works 20 hours a week at minimum wage will earn $145 a week; a full-time worker will earn $290. That works out to $580 a month ($145 multiplied by four weeks) for the part-timer, and $1,160 per month for the full-timer. To illustrate the financial impact of an employee on the bottom line, $1,160 has been added to the sample income and expense statement in this chapter, which could represent either a single full-time worker or two part-timers.

**Taxes:** For every wage earner on the payroll, there is an unavoidable tax liability that will — if you will pardon the pun— further tax your ability to meet payroll. Among the payroll taxes you must pay as the employer of record are: social security taxes (currently at 6.2 percent); Medicare taxes (1.45 percent); federal unemployment tax, a.k.a. FUTA (6.2 percent, unless you pay state unemployment insurance, which makes you eligible for a tax credit of up to 5.4 percent); workers' compensation (an amount determined by your state); and state unemployment tax (a.k.a. SUTA, an amount that also varies by state).

Here is how the monthly taxes would stack up for that single full-time employee mentioned above:

- **Social security taxes:** $71.92
- **Medicare taxes:** $16.82
- **FUTA:** $9.28 (assuming you qualify for the full SUTA discount rate)

Now, let us say you are doing business in the state of Washington. The SUTA tax in that fair state in 2009 was anywhere from 0 to 5.4 percent. If you are unlucky enough to have to pay the full 5.4 percent, that equates to another $62.64 in taxes on your full-time employee.

If you would like to investigate the rates for your state further, contact its unemployment tax agency. You can find a list of these state agencies at **www.business.gov/finance/taxes/state.html**.

Workers' comp rates are trickier to calculate. They vary by state and generally are assessed based on business type and a risk-factor classification code. A casual Internet survey showed that there usually is not a rate specifically for car detailers, meaning the tax amount likely is bundled into another automotive classification. For example, in Washington state, the closest classification is Auto Body Repair Centers, for which the composite base rate in 2009 was 1.1767 percent, or another $13.65 for the sample full-time employee discussed in this chapter.

So here are the bottom-line monthly wage and tax expenses for that single employee in Washington, which you will find noted in the sample income/expense statement:

- **Wages:** $1,160
- **Taxes (combined):** $174.31
- **Total:** $1,334.31

If you price your full detailing package at $100, that employee would have to do 13.34 full details every month for you just to break even on his or her salary and taxes. Assuming there are approximately 24 business days per month if your business is open six days a week, that 13.34 figure not only can be reached; it easily can be exceeded. But if you have a slow month, you could find yourself in a heap of trouble because you also will be drawing a salary of your own that will further erode your business's monthly income.

You can tell from all these figures, differences, and exceptions that it is a good idea to makes friends with an experienced accountant as soon as possible. You also may want to review IRS Publication 15, *Employer's Tax Guide*, which contains information on Social Security and Medicare tax. It is available at **www.irs. gov/publications/p15/index.html**.

Even if you do hire an accountant to help crunch the numbers and keep you out of trouble with Uncle Sam — which is recommended — you should keep your own running totals of how your business is doing on a monthly basis. An accounting software program such as QuickBooks is a good choice because it is inexpensive, easy to use, and customizable to your particular business situation. In a pinch, you can even use a program such as Excel, which is part of the bundled Microsoft® Office package, to tally up income and expenses, but you will have to create your own spreadsheets to do the job. With QuickBooks, you can choose from various templates and spend your off hours on tasks other than creating custom spreadsheets.

## Owner salary

Some entrepreneurs choose not to take a salary in the formative years of their businesses, opting instead to plow all the profits back into the business to increase its chances of success. But because most people tend to spend frivolously on, say, food and mortgage payments, it is more likely that you will need to draw a salary to keep your personal bills paid and your marriage or other personal relationships intact. For the sake of illustration, a modest owner salary of $2,000 per month is factored into the sample income/expense statement. Taxes of $306 also appear on the worksheet, which represent the federal self-employment tax of 15.3 percent. This tax consists of both halves of the social security and Medicare taxes, which you must pay for the privilege of being your own boss.

## Benefits

Offering fringe benefits such as health insurance, vacation time, sick pay, and retirement plans is a wonderful way to attract and retain good employees. But the reality is that you probably will not be able to afford to provide such perks so early in your new career. The U.S. Bureau of Labor Statistics says that the average cost per hour of such benefits is a whopping 29.2 percent. For this reason, no benefits costs are on the sample income/ expense statement.

## Monthly service charges

Mortgage and rent payments and personnel costs certainly will eat up the largest share of your monthly expense budget, so the monthly operational charges you will incur may look positively miniscule in comparison. Among these costs, all of which are estimated on the sample income/expenses statement, will be:

**Telecommunications:** This includes the cost of landlines for voice and fax communication, as well as cellular service. Even if you are starting a mobile-detailing business or an operation based in your garage, do not make your cell phone do double duty as both a personal and a business line. You really must have a dedicated business phone to appear professional, and a landline with voicemail capability usually is best. If you do not want a traditional landline, at the very least spring for a second cell-phone line that you can dedicate strictly to the business.

**Online charges:** These include the cost of online service — preferably broadband because it is the fastest — and Web-hosting charges. If you plan to engage the services of a Webmaster or content manager to help keep your Web site up-to-date and optimized, include the hourly cost of his or her services here, too.

**Accounting services:** It is safe to estimate that you will require the services of a qualified accountant or bookkeeper for a couple of hours a month, both to keep track of your accounts receivables and payables and to make sure the business taxes and tax filings are submitted on time.

**Legal services:** Most fledgling detailing-business owners will not need to have an attorney on retainer because detailing is a fairly low-liability business. Still, you never know when an employee might damage the finish on a prized vehicle, or when a customer might slip and fall in your shop. As a result, allocate funds every month — even if they are only on paper and will lounge comfortably in your bank account — in the event that you do need an attorney's services. A modest figure such as $50 to $100 a month should suffice.

**Merchant account:** A merchant account is an inescapable necessity for even the smallest detailing company because of today's credit/debit-dependent society. While it is not unheard of for a client to whip out a couple of crisp Benjamins to pay for a full detailing job, he or she is more likely to break out the plastic at the service counter (or in the parking lot, if you are a mobile detailer). Among the litany of fees associated with a merchant account are a transaction fee, processing fee, Internet gateway fee, retail discount fee, charge-back fee, statement fee, and probably more that have not been invented yet — it is good to be a merchant account provider. Rather than bore you with a bunch of calculated estimates, the sample income/expense statement includes a monthly fee of $40, with the caveat that this figure might be conservative.

**Check verification service:** Society has been moving toward plastic and away from proffering checks as payment. But if you are doing business in an area where checks still rule, you need to have this service, which verifies that a check will not bounce all the way to the bank. The fees for this service are similar to those of a merchant account.

**Advertising and promotion:** This figure can be a little difficult to calculate unless you have given some thought to the types of advertising you want to do to launch your business and promote it on an ongoing basis. At the very least, you will need to allocate funds to cover the cost of business cards, service brochures, direct mail pieces, fliers, and newspaper advertising. The cost of your Yellow Pages display ad and grand opening event, if you choose to have one, also can go here. The sample worksheet has a modest figure of $100 plugged in, but you may need to spend more to saturate your market.

## Transportation

Include the cost of gasoline and vehicle maintenance in your monthly estimate. This applies whether you are a mobile detailer who will take your mobile "shop" right to the customer, or a home-based detailer who will offer pick-up and drop-off service. Other costs to include are oil changes, tune-ups, and even windshield wiper fluid, as well as the percentage of your vehicle payment that you can attribute to business use. Be sure to keep good records for the IRS, though — you will have to itemize all the vehicle costs on your business tax return, or on Schedule C if you are a sole proprietor. Pick up a mileage and expense logbook at an office superstore and keep it in your vehicle so you can note these costs immediately.

You are now in the home stretch on the debit side of the income/ expenses statement. A few more things to work into your monthly budget include:

## Supplies

**Detailing supplies:** Your supply of carnauba wax, clay bars, paper floor mats, chamois, and even paper towels for the shop bathroom and coffee for the waiting-room coffeemaker must be replenished. Pick a nice, round figure — say, $200 a month — and you always will have enough cash on hand to cover these necessary expenses.

**Office supplies:** If you lay in a stockpile of office supplies such as paper, pens, folders, and so on when you launch the business, you probably will not need to buy much every month. But it still pays to allocate at least a nominal amount of money each month for those office-superstore spending sprees. About $50 a month should be enough.

**Postage:** Earmark sufficient funds for any mailings you plan to do to drum up new business, mail out invoices, and the like. Setting aside $440 a month would pay for 1,000 first-class mailing pieces, although your actual mailing volume is sure to ebb and flow with the seasons.

## Miscellaneous

This catch-all category is a good place to stash funds for magazine subscriptions, dues for professional organizations, and insurance premiums. Just tally up the annual cost of all these miscellaneous items, divide the bottom line total by 12, and add this amount to the monthly expense sheet. It also is a good idea to pad the final total with an extra 10 percent to cover miscellaneous expenses you do not yet know about.

Finally, if you must borrow money to finance the business, you should have a line item on your monthly income/expense statement where you note the repayment amount.

# Forecasting Income

Back in Chapter 1, you read a discussion of the earning potential for new detailing-business owners. You might want to review that information now to get a feel for how much you personally might expect to earn because you will need an estimate for your income/expense statement. If you are not certain how much to estimate, consider that Detail King, a leader in the detailing equipment, supply, and training world, says that the average cost of a detail service that includes machine polishing and interior detailing is $125 per vehicle. Sell a few extra services to each customer, such as paintless dent repair or engine detailing, and you significantly increase the per-vehicle profit.

So let us say that, in a day, you can reasonably complete two complete detailing jobs as described above. If you detail two cars 24 days a month (a pace equal to a six-day work week), you could earn $6,000 a month. Now, it is possible you will not be able to achieve this pace right from day one, so it might be a good idea to estimate a little lower (say, one vehicle a day for 24 days, or $3,000). You also have to take into consideration the fact that the geographical area where you will do business has a bearing on what you can charge. And, of course, if you have one employee or several who can help you buff and polish, you will be able to turn out even more vehicles each day and ratchet up the daily output figure even further.

A figure of $3,000 is on the sample income/expense statement to show you how the projected expenses discussed earlier in this chapter will impact the bottom line.

## CASE STUDY: MONEY MATTERS

Anthony Duva
A and A Duva Business Consulting
1541 Harvard St., Suite E
Santa Monica, CA 90404

Business consultant Anthony Duva has helped many first-time business owners get started in a variety of businesses, including car detailing. He says new entrepreneurs universally face the same challenges, any of which can make or break their business.

One of those universal challenges is a lack of cash flow.

"Insufficient cash flow is the killer of any business venture, large or small," Duva said. "You need enough cash coming in to pay for what you need, from payroll to electric bills to supplies. If you don't have enough cash flow, then money will be coming constantly from your own pocket. It is true that you will have to pay for everything in the start-up phase, but once the business is open, there should be some cash coming in to pay for the necessities, so the amount coming out of your pocket will go down."

The cost of capital is another common obstacle for a new business owner. If you cannot self-capitalize, it is not enough just to land a loan; you also have to recognize that capital costs will eat into your profits.

"You would be surprised how often the cost of capital is overlooked by business owners as a real business expense," Duva said. "If you borrow $1,000 and the interest rate is 10 percent, then you now owe an extra $100, which must be paid for directly out of your cash flow. If you cannot pay for the money you borrow, you will go under. There is no way around this."

Duva said a good rule of thumb when starting a business is to have at least enough cash on hand to cover six months to one year of projected expenses, plus start-up costs.

"You need enough cash on hand to ride out the bumps during the start-up phase. That way, you can survive while the business grows organically, and until it is self-supporting," he said.

Good marketing is also crucial for a successful business operation.

"All business owners should understand marketing," Duva said. "It is a broad term, but it really comes down to letting people know you are around and how they can find you. The problem is, many small-business owners tend to cut the marketing budget in bad times. This is a big mistake because if people cannot find you, they will not use your services, and those bad times will never get better. You can cut back on marketing, but you must never ignore it."

In the same way, you should not ignore the need for an accountant to guide you through the start-up phase and help manage your money.

"Accountants are a necessary evil," Duva said. "If there were no taxes, there would be no accountants, so use them because you need them."

Choosing a good location for the business also is crucial. Duva recommended establishing a location across the street from a high-volume business such as Burger King, The Coffee Bean & Tea Leaf, or Starbucks. Think of it this way: Those companies spend millions of dollars in location research before they allow a new franchise to open. Capitalize on their knowledge and open up near the popular brands. The hope is that when customers come out of those stores with their coffee or burgers in hand, they will see your shop across the way and will remember it when they need detailing services. Better still, set up a cross-promotion with one of the franchises. Try offering a small percentage off a detailing job, top off a customer's windshield washing fluid for free, or offer an inexpensive promotional item (such as a free keychain) to customers to induce them to cross the road to get to you.

Attracting business is certainly important, but you must have the right employees in place to handle the business, Duva said. Although you can advertise for employees the old-fashioned way, it is also a good idea to look for help through Internet job searches. Then, when you do find employees, treat them right.

"Most employees will stay with a job if they have a sense of satisfaction and a feeling of accomplishment when their work is done," Duva said. Train them, talk to them, and listen to their ideas, and you will have a more satisfied crew, he said.

With the poor state of the economy in recent years, this might not seem like a very good time to start a business. But Duva disagrees.

"If you have some money saved and you can ride out the bad times, you will be perfectly situated to be part of the coming recovery," he said. "Just remember that most business owners only get one chance. You can improve your chances of success if you manage your money well and do your homework. Just as a player does not learn to play baseball in the World Series, you do not learn how to run your business *after* you have opened the doors."

# Financing the Dream

If you intend to start small and modestly, you should be able to keep your start-up expenses low and hopefully pay for them solely from personal savings. Notice the phrase "personal savings" — that is always preferable to financing what you need. But if you truly have no financial reserves, and your start-up expenses are low, then plastic is the way to go. Just be very careful about how much you spend. There is no question that it is fun and exhilarating to skip up and down the aisles of the auto superstore, merrily slam-dunking supplies and equipment into your cart. But financial liabilities have the tendency to weigh down even the most careful business owner, so pay for your supplies and equipment out of pocket if at all possible.

Besides tapping savings accounts, you might consider using other personal cash reserves such as certificates of deposit, stocks and bonds, savings bonds, and retirement funds, such as IRAs, 401(k) plans, and SEPs. You also can sell real estate, jewelry, and vehicles to raise cash.

Of course, if you will be running a much larger operation, then financing may be inevitable. Here are some sources of financing that are worth a look:

**Friends and family:** Ah, the people who love you could be a gold mine of start-up cash. But if you manage to convince them that you deserve their backing, make sure you handle the transaction professionally. That means drawing up a promissory note for each lender that details the terms of the loan and a repayment schedule. Sign off on the paperwork and give each lender a copy. Then stick to the repayment schedule. The last thing you want to do is sink a friendship or estrange family members because you have broken the terms of the contract. If you cannot pay back the loan as expected, discuss the situation with your lenders and come to a new agreement.

**Investors:** The more money you need, the more likely it is that you will need investors rather than just lenders. Investors, however, get a percentage of your business in exchange for their stake in the operation, which in turn reduces your ownership stake. Some small-business owners turn first to friends and family to find prospective investors, but depending on the financial stake you need, you may need to look elsewhere. Your financial institution, attorney, or accountant may be able to direct you to potential investors, as can the professional organizations you belong to. Sometimes just putting out the word that you are looking for business investors is enough to generate interest in your venture.

**Financial institutions:** If you have a positive and long-standing relationship with a bank or credit union, you might want to make it your first stop on the road to business financing. Usually, a small community bank is more likely to be receptive to a financing pitch because of its commitment to the town it serves. Even so, it can be challenging to pry loose any cash during an economic downturn. Your friendly local credit union also could be a potential source of funding. Credit-union lending standards tend to be a little looser than those of banks; plus, these institutions usually often offer better rates to their members. There is a credit union for practically every type of organization and worker, from churches and educational institutions, to dairy employees and electricians (two favorites: The Jackson Vibrators Employees Credit Union in Ludington, Michigan, and the American Hammered Federal Credit Union in Baltimore, Maryland). For a list of credit unions nationwide, go to **www.creditunionsonline.com**.

**Home equity loans/lines of credit:** During the historic recession of the past few years, home values have plummeted precipitously, and consumer lending has tightened up considerably. But if you have stellar credit and a significant amount of equity, your bank or credit union still may be willing to listen to you. Many financial institutions, however, take a dim view of using home equity for a business start-up. Still, it is worth asking about — just be sure to have a Plan B in case you are turned down flatly.

**Small Business Administration (SBA):** This government organization is the place to go if the lender you approach will not approve your loan, which usually happens because a new business is considered to be a risky venture. The SBA itself does not actually lend money, but it does offer a loan guaranty program, in which it backs up to 85 percent of a small-business loan. The traditional lender works on the loan request with the nearest SBA district office, then the SBA analyzes the loan application and decides whether to back the request. Among the requirements for an SBA-backed loan are that the business must be run for profit and must meet certain size standards. You also must submit a boatload of paperwork as part of the application. The lending institution remains in the financial picture all the way because it is responsible for closing the loan, ponying up the cash, and collecting your payments down the road.

SBA loans can be lifesavers for fledgling entrepreneurs, but they are not without disadvantages. To begin with, such loans usually have higher interest rates than standard bank loans. Also, in some cases you may have to provide a lot more documentation than the bank normally requires — plus, it can take longer to get approved because the wheels of government do tend to turn slowly. Some prospective small-business owners are put off by the government hoops they must jump through, but if an SBA-backed loan is your only option, the extra requirements may be worth the trouble.

**Other options:** The Internet is teeming with companies that specialize in providing unsecured loans to small-business owners. But *caveat emptor:* They often charge towering fees and have exorbitant interest rates. If you have no other choice than to try one of these companies, investigate it thoroughly, starting with a search of its Better Business Bureau rating. Get everything in writing and have your attorney look over the paperwork. Forewarned is forearmed, as the saying goes.

Finally, a less scary way to get the equipment you need for your business is to turn to the auto-detailing experts for financing. Among those that offer financing are Detail Plus, the company owned by RL "Bud" Abraham in Portland, Oregon, and Detail King in Pittsburgh, Pennsylvania.

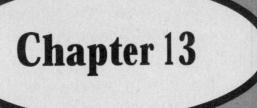

# Chapter 13

## Approaching the Finish Line

Before wrapping up this discussion of the tasks you need to undertake to launch your car detailing business, it is important to consider two final things that will be crucial to your success. The first, environmental sustainability, refers to adopting a responsible approach to meeting your current needs without harming the environment, thus ensuring that subsequent generations will be able to meet their own needs. This is particularly important for a car detailer. Many of the things you will do in the course of performing your job will have an environmental impact, from using power tools with high decibel levels to accidentally allowing water contaminated with soap and chemicals to leach into the groundwater. It will be up you to promote environmental sustainability on a daily basis. Luckily, this is not hard, nor — in most cases — expensive to do.

The second thing left to consider is personal enrichment. Certainly, earning a living doing something you love provides plenty of that, but you can enrich yourself even more by doing things to improve your skills and help you become the best car detailer and small-business owner possible. Such things include pursuing educational opportunities, joining professional and allied organizations, and keeping abreast of news that impacts the industry (including those environmental sustainability issues mentioned above).

Therefore, this chapter covers both the simple steps you can take to be more eco-friendly, as well as professional development possibilities and opportunities. *Contact information for the educational providers, organizations, publications, and other companies named in this chapter can be found in Appendix E.*

# Protecting the Earth

Car detailers often come under fire from municipalities, environmental groups, and neighbors for their unwanted and sometimes noxious discharges into wastewater systems and the groundwater — and with good reason. Soaps, chemicals, and "gray water," which is tap water contaminated by soap and other nontoxic residue, all take a toll on the planet when inappropriately discharged. For this reason, the car detailing industry has come up with various types of products and equipment to lessen this impact and make the industry more environmentally sustainable. Some of them include:

## Green detailing products

When you wash and clean vehicles for a living, you inevitably will use a lot of water. But you can reduce that amount and still do your job well; try using waterless or dry-wash products. You still must mix these super-concentrated products with water (usually in a 10:1 dilution), plus you may want to wet each section of the vehicle as you apply the product. But in the end you will use far less water than the 80 to 140 gallons of water the International Car Wash Association estimates for a typical hand-wash. A few waterless car-wash products to try include Detail King Dry Wash Spray Polish (**www.detailking.com**); Eco Touch Waterless Car Wash (**http://ecotouch.net**); and Rejuvenate Auto 15-Minute Waterless Car Wash (**www.rejuvenateauto.com**). Some dry-wash products even contain nonhazardous polymer resins and carnauba wax to protect the vehicle after "washing," and you can use them even if you will be buffing the vehicle. Go-Green Waterless Wash by Chemical Guys (**www.chemicalguys.com**) is one product to try. A 1-gallon jug will help restore up to 70 vehicles to showroom condition.

"Green" buffing products also can help reduce your environmental footprint. Manufacturers have learned how to reduce the number of solvents in their detailing products, which in turn yields products that will not harm you, the vehicle, or the environment during use. Kleen Car Auto Appearance (**www.1car detailing-training.com**) has a line of environmentally safe products that warrant consideration.

Other companies that produce plant-based green detailing products that are nontoxic, biodegradable, and earth-friendly include Car Planet (**www.carplanetdetailing.com**), Green Earth Technologies (**www.getg.com**), and Zymöl (**www.zymol.com**).

# Eco-friendly equipment

Pressure washers are great for exterior and engine cleaning, but they use a lot of water — and cold water, to boot. So eco-savvy detailers have started using steam pressure washers to blast off dirt, rail and brake dust, road tar, and other contaminants. The powerful Therma-Kleen Steam Machine (**www.thermakleen. com**) has a maximum steam temperature of 340 degrees Fahrenheit to handle even the dirtiest vehicles, all without damaging their painted exterior. It is compact enough for a mobile detailer to have on board. But best of all for the environment, this steamer has virtually no water run-off.

Another well-known steam-washer brand is the Daimer Super Max® 6000 or 7000 (**www.daimer.com**). Daimer also offers its own line of bio-based, green products that include car and truck wash, carpet and upholstery cleaner, and even windshield washer fluid.

# Waste-reclamation and disposal equipment

As you may recall, back in Chapter 6 it was suggested that every new mobile detailer invest in a water-reclamation system. The simplest of these systems is actually quite low-tech, consisting of a containment mat, a vacuum for capturing gray water, and a holding tank for storing the wastewater until it can be recycled. The idea is, of course, to keep that gray water out of the storm drains. That is important because in addition to soap, gray water contains the residue from the detailing products or chemicals you have used, as well as any oil, tar, brake dust, and other road contaminants you have washed off. Detail Plus offers a full line of containment mats (**www.detailplus.com**).

Mobile detailers most commonly have a containment system as described above, although in a pinch, a tarp and a wet/dry vacuum will do (although only when used on a level surface). Another more professional system that works well is Vacu-Boom (**www. vacuboom.com**). It consists of several flexible tube-like sections that are placed on concrete or asphalt, then tightly sealed to the surface to form a water-containment area. You use a vacuum to collect the water after the detailing job is complete.

But containing the water is only the first step; proper disposal is crucial to protect the environment. If gray water is contaminated only by biodegradable soap, it usually is safe to discharge it into landscaped areas because plants actually like the nitrogen and low levels of phosphorus it contains. Just be sure to get the homeowner's permission first; do not dump too much water in the same spot; and never recycle water that contains too many pollutants, such as road tar.

The most ecologically sound thing to do is to dispose of gray water in a proper sanitary sewer, which is the same pipeline used to carry away sewage from the toilet. Unless you plan to dump the water into your home sanitary sewer, you will have to make other arrangements. One idea to try: Strike a deal with the local self-serve car wash to pay a small fee to discharge water into its sanitary sewer. Better still, if you are detailing on the premises of a business with a sanitary sewer, such as an auto dealership, ask for permission to access the sanitary sewer, and the problem is solved.

Speaking of obtaining permission, if you do plan to use your home sanitary sewer, always check first with your local municipality. It likely will have many regulations and restrictions on the practice.

Incidentally, a sanitary sewer is different from a storm sewer in two important ways. First, it is used to convey human waste and other heavy waste away from homes and businesses, whereas a storm sewer simply carries away water from precipitation. Second, when installed in a business that discharges a lot of contaminated water (including car washes and car detailing shops), it must have an oil/water/sand separator installed between the drain and the sewer. The separator screens out oil and other sludge before the water enters the sewer. From there, the water goes to a sewage-treatment plant to be sanitized, then eventually makes its way back into streams and rivers. A sanitary sewer is a great, eco-friendly system — but at $50,000, it is not something a mobile dealer would ever choose to install. Naturally, if you are starting a site-based detailing company, you definitely *will* be required to have a working oil/water/sand separator on your sewer line.

If you are tempted to pour your car-washing water and sludge into the storm drain, remember that the EPA takes a dim view of businesses that violate the Federal Clean Water Act that way. Water that goes into the storm drain is returned to rivers, streams, and lakes without any treatment. As a result, wash water and other non-storm water introduced into storm drains can cause environmentally hazardous conditions.

If you think you will not get caught dumping contaminated water, think again. All it takes is a disgruntled neighbor or business owner to turn you in. So to stay out of the EPA's crosshairs and avoid towering fines, find a legal way to dump or recycle your wastewater.

# Empowering Yourself to Succeed

Author and professional development guru Anthony J. D'Angelo has said, "Never stop learning; knowledge doubles every 14 months." This is the reason why it is so important to keep your skills current and your knowledge base up-to-date.

Now, this is not suggesting you get a business degree — although that definitely will help you be a more savvy business owner. It is not even saying you should spend hundreds or even thousands of dollars on car detailing education — although that will help you become a better detailer. Instead, grab every opportunity that presents itself to learn more about your profession and your craft. The following are some easy ways to do that.

## Back to school, detailing style

If you have been detailing for a while, either by working for someone else or by keeping your own ride polished and pretty, you probably will not need a basic primer on how to clean and buff. But if you are a car enthusiast with no experience who now wishes to detail for a living, you may need some professional help. Several of the car detailing product and equipment companies mentioned in this book offer training that can be just what Dr. Auto ordered. Some have on-site training at their own facility, while some detailing consultants will travel to your home turf to impart their wisdom. The latter is far more expensive than the former, but if you have sufficient start-up funding, you might want to set aside some possibly tax-deductible bucks to learn from a pro. Check with your tax adviser to be sure about the deductibility.

Among the companies that offer instruction in detailing technique and/or business management are:

- Auto Detailing Institute
  (**www.autodetailinginstitute.com**)
- Detail In Progress (**www.detailinprogress.com**)
- Detail King (**www.detailking.com**)
- Detail Plus Car Appearance Systems
  (**www.detailplus.com**)
- Ding King Auto Detail School
  (**www.autodetail-school.com**)
- Kleen Car Auto Appearance
  (**www.1car detailing-training.com**)
- Rightlook (**www.rightlook.com**)

Other low-to-no-cost sources of training information are the Web sites of some of the product/equipment sellers, where you can view demos and possibly obtain DVDs and books at a nominal cost. If you cannot make it to a traditional training session, this is the next best thing. Finally, equipment and product companies may offer instruction on how to use their tools and products correctly and safely. Ask your regional representative about these opportunities.

For business-specific information, tap into the knowledge and resources of the Small Business Administration (**www.sba.gov**), which offers free help to small-business owners. Yet another source of free business information is SCORE (**www.score.org**), Known as the "Counselors to America's Small Business," SCORE offers free in-person and telephone mentoring and counseling, business workshops, and online assistance, all provided by volunteers who are active and retired executives. Last year alone, SCORE counselors assisted 8.5 million business owners. With 364 nationwide chapters, it probably has a location near you.

## Academic pursuits

When you decided to become a car detailer, you probably did not envision signing up for college classes. But you definitely will find that business classes at the local university or community college are valuable for learning what you need to know to manage your business better and more successfully. Many universities and colleges allow students to sit in on classes for no grade, a situation known as auditing. You do not even have to take the exams or turn in the papers and other assignments if you do not want to, although if you go to the trouble of signing up, paying the tuition, and attending class, you really should get with the program and do all the work, too. Business classes that are helpful for detailing-business owners include accounting, marketing, and advertising, to name just a few.

If college classes are really out of your comfort — or financial — zone, try taking a few business classes through the community education department of the local school district instead. Often, practitioners who really know their stuff teach these classes, and they generally are very inexpensive.

Finally, another easy way to find out what is new and exciting in car detailing is to attend a trade show for car-care professionals. Notice this did not say "detailing professionals" because, frankly, there is no show devoted strictly to detailing. But most trade shows and expositions devote part of their agenda to detailing issues. For example, the Midwest Carwash Association recently held a session at its annual expo on how to develop and operate a successful detailing business, both in a car wash and as a fixed site/mobile business. You may be able to attend such a session even if you are not a member of the organization. Call the show office to see if you can obtain an invitation.

Other automotive-related shows with educational programs might be of interest, including the Specialty Equipment Marketing Association (SEMA) Show (**www.semashow.com**), which showcases automotive specialty products, including restoration products. You do have to be a member of SEMA to attend. Get the details at **www.sema.org**.

## Detailing organizations

Alas, there are no longer any associations strictly for car detailers. But there are a few auto-related organizations that have a detailing category among their membership ranks. One such organization is the International Carwash Association (**www.carwash.org**).

## Business organizations

It is always a good idea to get involved in the community where you work, both to gain visibility for your business and to establish and enhance your reputation as an ethical and civic-minded business person; just think of all the new customers, future employees, and business contacts you can meet this way. If available, always take advantage of an organization's networking and educational opportunities, and if possible, take a board member position to ramp up your visibility quotient. Good business organizations to join include the chamber of commerce, Rotary Club, and Soroptimist International. You also might want to consider joining the economic or business-development organization in your community or region.

Here is another good reason to join a civic organization: They often offer access to group health insurance and provide discounts and other valuable services to members.

## Publications, Web sites, blogs, and forums

The detailing industry may be short on dedicated organizations, but there definitely is no shortage of information on the profession. One of the leading publications for detailing information is *Professional Carwashing & Detailing*, which is available free to qualified car wash and detailing professionals at **www.carwash. com**. While you are there, sign up for the two free e-newsletters, *Professional Carwashing & Detailing e-News* and *Professional Detailing eNews*. Another publication you might find of interest is *Modern Car Care* (**www.moderncarcare.com**), which regularly covers issues of importance to detailers.

Detailing Web sites are another great source of information. In addition to offering free e-newsletters, they dispense a wealth of information for novice and experienced detailers alike. Detailers also love to blog and post to bulletin boards. In addition to the blogs on **www.detailingsuccess.com** and **www.autodetailing-network.com**, have a look at the following blogs to find out what the pros are thinking:

- Detail City (**www.detailcity.org**) is a detailing organization that runs a lively bulletin board loaded with detailing threads

- Detailing Gurus (**www.blogcatalog.com/blog/detailing-gurus-auto-detailing-blog**)

- Detail King (**www.detailking.com/blog/home.php**) provides tons of detailing information, training, products, and equipment

- USCarDetailing (**http://usacardetailing.wordpress.com**), which actually is the blog site for Daimer; it has a sales slant, but it is a good place to read about detailing equipment

- Detail Plus (**www.detailplus.com/forum/signin.asp**), where you register with your e-mail and a password and can ask or view questions

Speaking of the pros, enter the term "detailing blogs" into an Internet search engine to get a large number of blogs posted by detailers just like you who have something to say. No doubt, these blogs are maintained for the benefit of the detailers' own customers, but they still are interesting to follow and learn from — and they may give you plenty of ideas for launching a blog for your own clientele eventually. Finally, detailing-product Web sites often dispense free information and offer online forums along with their pitches to buy their products and equipment.

CASE STUDY: DO YOUR
HOMEWORK

Robert Regan, The Auto Detailing Teacher
and Winner's Circle Towels Inc.
Santa Barbara, CA
Phone: 888-869-3576, 805-448-5132
E-mail: sales@wcdetail.com
Web site: www.autodetailingteacher.com

Robert Regan is a classic example of how a car detailer can take advantage of the many opportunities that present themselves in life and, as a result, build a thriving, multifaceted business.

An elementary teacher who holds a master's degree in education and still teaches full time, Regan founded The Auto Detailing Teacher, a mobile operation, in 1995. After a while, he diversified his detailing business by selling detailing products online. His next entrepreneurial venture was to import good-quality, affordable towels that also could be sold online. Today, with his wife, Susan, Regan operates his detailing shop, Winner's Circle Towels Inc., and its two subsidiaries, Winner's Circle Online and Towel Pros. The towels are sold mostly to detailers, car washes, and resellers, but Towel Pros' products also have the distinction of being the towel of choice for the detailers of Air Force One, as well as numerous high-end detailers nationwide.

As a school teacher who also trains aspiring detailers, it is not surprising that Regan's best advice to detailing neophytes revolves around learning as much about the industry as possible. Toward that end, he recommends educating yourself, interviewing successful detail-business owners, attending trade shows, and networking as much as possible.

He also says that proper marketing is of paramount importance. He admits that in the beginning, he personally had some difficulties marketing his business to the middle-income customers and the occasional higher-income clients he now serves.

"I thought it would be easy if I just put an ad in the paper and listened for the phone to ring," Regan said. "Not so — this is a service that many are still unaware of, even today, and are still slow to accept. Customer education has been my best method of advertising."

By taking the time to educate customers about the importance of good car care, Regan has accrued a client base consisting of "maintenance detail" customers, who come in for regularly scheduled detailing jobs. He also has many regular customers who have their vehicles detailed just once a year. But to stay viable when the economy is slow, he offers an express-detail special for $79.99. It makes more money per hour for the business than some other jobs and, because it is not as intense or involved, it is more economical for the customer.

After learning the hard way that newspaper advertising is not a particularly fruitful source of new business, Regan now uses low-cost local discount-shopper publications, has a Yellow Pages ad, and counts on positive word-of-mouth advertising.

"I am still working on making my business as successful as it can be," Regan said. "What has given me a very loyal following is the training I have undertaken. I am certified by a detail training [program] and can talk about paint care in a way that almost no one in my area can match. That has made a difference. Customers seem pleased and surprised to learn about detailing from me and hear what is really involved."

Like many other detailers, Regan is aware that there is more scrutiny these days by local cities when it comes to detailing businesses.

"There are still many 'fly-by-night' mobile operators running around with no insurance and so forth," he said. "That is frustrating because it brings a certain connotation to the industry that is not favorable."

This teacher recommends that anyone who wishes to start a detailing business should do his or her homework first.

"Don't assume that because you are a good detailer or car washer that you will just sit back and count your money," he said. "This is a hard business. Do market studies and know what you have to pay if you want the right equipment, training, and location. When selecting a location, observe traffic patterns in the area, and be aware of the speed limit and how easy it is to enter and exit the parking lot. These factors will all impact your business."

Although he has hired many employees over the years, Regan considers himself still in learning mode. But he does have some criteria that make it easier to pick good employees. For instance, a person who has a clean driving record is probably at least somewhat responsible. He also prefers not to hire anyone who has worked previously as a detailer, because such employees usually come in with preconceived notions of how to detail and do not want to adapt to Regan's personal style. Rather, he prefers people who are trainable and will follow the specific procedures that he knows will result in a more efficient detail.

"The main qualities an employee needs are conversational skills and a good personality," he added. "I also expect them to be clean, dress well, and listen well."

Pricing is another area where Regan does not compromise.

"I will adjust costs in some cases, but I always make sure I earn at least $50 per hour," he said. "This allows me to pay the bills, covers the cost of the five to six products used for each detail, and nets what I feel I need."

Of course, the price can increase in certain cases. For instance, if Regan has to use expensive equipment such as a vapor steamer, the price goes up. Likewise, if he knows he is going to get really dirty because he has to crawl around while detailing, that raises the price, too. On the other hand, if he is doing a detail-prep for a car show, he charges less because it is an easier job in terms of labor — plus, he gets word-of-mouth recognition from the show and customer.

Regan sees a bright future for the detailing industry but admits that not all business owners will survive.

"I think many will be out of business because they are not flexible, and they do not follow local regulations," he said. "In some cases, they lack a decent education and have poor grammar and speaking skills. Worse yet, they lack business skills and think that because they can detail a car, they can run a business. Then, months down the road, they find themselves in trouble with the city — or they are out of money."

Regan also predicts that more eco-friendly products and procedures will be used in the future and that pressure washers and water tanks will become almost obsolete in the next few years. He also foresees the development of vapor-steam technology, better towels, and other products that allow the shop to clean, polish, and protect vehicles quickly.

For now, Regan just likes to make sure his customers are happy. He pays special attention to making sure all the glass is polished perfectly, even though he says customers are more apt to notice how the paint and the carpet look when they see their detailed vehicle. Usually it is not until they have driven off that they realize how beautifully the glass has been maintained.

Regan's advice for start-up detailing entrepreneurs includes:

- *Get funded:* "Money is the key. If you do not have it, it is very hard to do this business the right way from the start."

- *Visit detailing shops and interview the owners:* See what works for other owners and how you can emulate their operational formula.

- *Involve the community in your market plan:* Regan gives 10 percent back to local schools and camps as a way to support the community and become a visible part of it. He also suggests working closely with the city where you do business and holding charitable events whenever you can. These are all ways to get people talking about you.

- *Do the math:* Determine how much you need to earn per man-hour to pay all the bills, then figure out your pricing.

- *Hold detailing clinics for the public:* Share some of your detailing tricks and pitch your products, and you will gain either new product sales or new detailing clients.

- *Advertise judiciously and often:* The average person needs to see an advertising message about seven to ten times before he or she will act or remember a business. Be consistent with your ad campaigns, and do not fret when you do not get a bunch of calls with one ad. It takes time to get results.

# Conclusion

## Start Your Engines

A nd there you have it: everything you need to know to launch a self-sustaining car detailing business in 13 easy chapters. Naturally, when it comes to detailing, a significant part of the learning experience will spring directly from the hands-on, dirt-under-your-nails work you will perform both inside and outside the vehicles you detail. Everything else — like learning how to market yourself or to create a profit-loss statement — can be learned over time. For that reason, we encourage you to speak to other detailers, join a few business associations, take some business courses, and otherwise make yourself and your business name known around town. Those are the surest ways to start on the road to detailing business success, and we wish you well on the journey.

# Appendix A

## The Sample Business Plan

The business plan that follows is representative of the type of plan needed by a small car detailing business. You may find that you will need to expand upon some of the sections in order to provide enough detail to prospective investors or bankers. But this is a good starting place for most detailing businesses.

### Front Cover

**Kenneth Russell Detailing**
*Details Are Our Business*
**September 2010**
**Confidential**
**Development Leader**

**Kenneth W. Russell**
**27249 Lawrence St. Chicago, IL 60640**
**Phone: 555-555-9999**
**Fax: 555-555-1234**
**Web site: www.kennethrusselldetailing.com**
**E-mail: contactken@kennethrusselldetailing.com**

## Executive Summary

Kenneth Russell Detailing (KRD) is an Illinois-based detailing company that will clean and care for vehicles in the Chicago region. These services will be targeted at customers with middle- to upper-level incomes. The purpose of this business plan is to outline the plans for opening and operating a vehicle-detailing shop, which will be located at 27249 Lawrence St. in Chicago, IL 60640 under the name Kenneth Russell Detailing. The objective of this business plan is to secure a $150,000 loan from a financial institution in order to purchase the facility and materials needed for start-up and ongoing operating costs for this business endeavor. An outline of the business's long-term marketing strategies is also included. KRD will be a limited liability company formed by Kenneth and Cathy Russell.

KRD will be a full-service detailing provider. Services will include maintenance and restorative services for the interior and exterior of vehicles ranging from passenger cars to light trucks, motorcycles, sport utility vehicles, vans, and more. Among those services will be standard vehicle maintenance services like hand-washing, vacuuming, and conditioning the interior of vehicles; and hand-washing, waxing, and polishing the exterior. Engine and trunk detailing will also be part of the standard maintenance service. Restorative services will include paintless dent removal (PDR), paint touch-up, overspray and rail dust removal, black trim restoration, paint sealant application, upholstery treatment, and windshield chip repair.

Services will be rendered on-site in a 5,000-square-foot facility, or at customers' homes and/or workplaces using a mobile detailing rig. Initial staffing needs will be three full-time technicians and one or two part-time technicians who would be used on a seasonal basis. The co-owners and a full-time shop manager round out the personnel needed to run the business.

The business also will have an on-site gift shop/store that will sell auto-themed merchandise and detailing products. The shop will offer a line of proprietary eco-friendly detailing products sold under the "Ken's Totally Green Detailing" name.

The initial funding request for this business is $150,000. Additional funding of up to $25,000 per year for three years also is requested to continue the research and development of additional eco-friendly detailing products.

## Objectives

KRD will give customers unique and personalized service from every standpoint. In the shop interacting with store associates, online, or on the telephone, we can answer any questions customers might have about our services. Customers also can take part in surveys so we can improve our service every day, and we will encourage customers to give us suggestions about items they would like to see added to our already comprehensive list of services. Customized detailing services will be our specialty, and we will strive to stand out above the competition. Services can be done in-store or at the customer's home or place of employment.

Orders for detailing and auto-related merchandise will be accepted as customers browse our Web site at their leisure in their home. Nationally, we will help customers find the right detail shop while on the road, and we will do the legwork to find it for them if necessary.

KRD is truly committed to making sure customers walk away satisfied and with a more thorough knowledge of what is involved in the entire car detailing process and how they can benefit from this knowledge.

## Mission

It is the mission of KRD to give every customer an excellent customer-service experience, no matter how large or small the detailing job. We will offer a creative and personal approach and encourage customers to watch and understand the process of cleaning and detailing their cars. Sales associates are not only employees at KRD, but customer service representatives who are dedicated to the company's overall success. They will be trained to do the best detailing job possible, and will be encouraged to know customers on a personal level. This, in turn, will give both customers and employees a unique comfort level, which is needed for customers to ask questions, thus enabling them to have a better understanding of what their car needs are now and will be in the future.

## Keys to Success

The keys to success for KRD include the following:

- Give customers an exceptional job and thorough under-standing of the car detailing shop services and processes for their cars.

- Foster a professional relationship with each customer in an effort to ensure he/she is given exceptional service and is pleased with the results of the detailing work.

- Cater to customers' needs. Strive to go the extra mile to meet and go beyond customer expectations at all times.

- Get to know clients on a first-name basis and remember the cars they drive and their needs. The intention is to be able to suggest new services as they are introduced in the shop.

- Continue to give customers an exceptional and unique experi-ence to keep their business for years to come.

## Statement of Purpose

KRD's business plan has been created to obtain money for the busi-ness in the amount of $150,000, which will be used for both start-up costs and ongoing operational costs. This business plan also serves to give potential investors a complete idea about plans for the com-pany's future development, which could include expansion into other states in the United States, and possibly in other countries, as well.

## Company Summary

KRD will be a full-service detailing provider. Services will include maintenance and restorative services for the interior and exterior of vehicles ranging from passenger cars to light trucks, motorcycles, sport utility vehicles, vans, and more. As the business grows, it is the owners' intention to expand into detailing commercial vehicles, but at this time, it is likely that KRD will service only the occasional commercial truck or van.

KRD will feature an on-site gift shop with car-themed merchandise like greeting cards, key chains, travel mugs, and vehicle ornaments (such as leather steering-wheel covers). The shop also will carry a line of consumer detailing and car wash products. Chief among them will be an eco-friendly product line, patented by company owners Kenneth and Cathy Russell, called "Ken's Totally Green Detailing."

KRD will take the customer service aspect of the business to an even higher level by offering a unique locator service, which will allow us to help our customers online and by telephone locate reliable detailing services whenever they are traveling outside our own region. The company also will offer online appointment booking and convenient vehicle pick-up and delivery services for work that will be done both in the shop and detailing at the customer's home or workplace.

KRD employees will be trained to listen carefully to customers' concerns, then counsel them personally on the services needed to restore their vehicle to showroom or near-showroom condition. Employees will be fully informed about the car wash and detailing products KRD sells so they can make educated suggestions to customers and thus increase the price point of every sale. Customers who use the pick-up and delivery service will be able to shop online and have products delivered to them when their vehicle is finished, thus saving on delivery costs.

Customer comfort in the shop also will be of paramount importance. The waiting room will feature a big-screen TV, plus there will be a live feed on a separate monitor showing technicians at work on customers' vehicles. Also, a computer with an interactive program will allow customers to browse car-related information, pull up tips on cosmetic vehicle maintenance, and read ways to extend the life of a car's exterior and interior.

## Company Ownership

Kenneth Russell, co-owner of Kenneth Russell Detailing, has been in the detailing and car wash business for the past 20 years. He graduated with a bachelor's degree in business management from the University of Texas at Austin and has always enjoyed working with cars and people. After graduation, Russell worked in various detail shops in Texas and New York before moving to Chicago, where he opened his first detailing business, a small shop that was formed as a sole proprietorship. That shop will be replaced by the larger shop that will be called Kenneth Russell Detailing.

Cathy Russell, co-owner of Kenneth Russell Detailing, has a degree in biology and chemistry. She is a chemist who was responsible for the development of the business's eco-friendly product line. With her husband, Ken, she holds the patent on these products and continues to work to create additional green detailing products that will meet the standards of the future.

## Company Management and Organization

The company management will consist of co-owners Kenneth W. Russell and Cathy Russell, and a full-time shop manager to be hired later.

We anticipate hiring three full-time technicians and one or two part-time technicians who will be used on a seasonal basis.

## Company Location and Facility

Kenneth Russell Detailing will be located at 27249 Lawrence St., Chicago, IL 60640. Phone: 555-555-9999; Web site: www.kenrusselldetailing.com; and e-mail: contactken@kennethrusselldetailing.com.

## Legal Form of Business

The legal name of the business is Kenneth Russell Detailing, and it will operate as a partnership, as registered in the state of Illinois.

## Services

As a full-service car detail shop, KRD will offer a full slate of standard vehicle maintenance services, including hand-washing, vacuuming, and conditioning the interior of vehicles; and hand-washing, waxing, and polishing the exterior. Engine and trunk detailing will also be part of the standard maintenance service. Restorative services will include paintless dent removal (PDR), paint touch-up, overspray and rail dust removal, black trim restoration, paint sealant application, upholstery treatment, and windshield chip repair. Eventually, Ken's will add gold trim restoration to its service menu to cater to upscale customers in the Chicago metropolitan area.

Customers who drive in will choose the level of service they would like for their cars. Car detail technicians will always be on hand to answer any questions about the products used, many of which are proprietary eco-friendly products. We also will offer a "frequent buyer" program that rewards customers for repeat business.

Beyond the standard services, KRD will offer traditional detailing services at customers' homes or offices. Clients can choose to have a professional driver pick up and return deliver their vehicle to the location of their choice, or customers can elect to have their vehicles serviced on-site by a trained mobile detailer. Services can be booked through our Web site or by phone from anywhere in the continental United States. This includes booking services even when a client is out of KRD's service area. We will help customers find a shop near their location, then call the shop and make the appointment. While there is no financial reward for KRD to offer such a service, what it does is build recognition for our brand and increase customer satisfaction.

Product purchases will also be expedited for KRD's customers. Products may be ordered online and shipped by Priority Mail® for speedy delivery. Alternatively, customers who are already scheduled for detailing services can order products online and have them ready for pick-up or delivery when their vehicle is ready. This will save customers the cost of shipping and further increase customer satisfaction. A truly unique service KRD will offer is the application of temporary vehicle artwork or written messages for special occasions. For example, we can professionally hand-letter messages on wedding party vehicles or vehicles that will be used in a parade. All products used for such lettering or artwork are environmentally friendly and will not damage the car's exterior. The cost of removing the lettering or artwork after the event will be included in the price, and can be done either in our facility or the customer's home or office.

## Market Analysis Summary

According to a statistics compiled by IBISWorld, a business information provider, car wash and detailing industry revenue was $8.05 million in 2009. Due to the economic slowdown of the past decade, industry revenues have declined slightly, but it is predicted that revenues will stabilize and grow again thanks to increased environmental awareness. It is expected that as the economy strengthens, customers will again rely on both car washes and detailers to keep their vehicles clean while conserving water. With a strengthening of the economy will come an increase in disposable income, which also will increase the likelihood that consumers will use detailing services. While there are hundreds of car washes/detailing shops already in operation in the Chicago metropolis, KRD will be located in an affluent area with a population of around 200,000 people that currently is served by only one other detailer. That detailer services vehicles of all makes and years. By focusing its attention on higher-end brands — although not to the exclusion of everyday models — KRD will be able to command the luxury vehicle market.

Another thing KRD will do to set itself apart from the other car washes/detailing shops in its target market is offer its line of patented eco-friendly detailing and car washing products. In addition, at the present time KRD will be one of just two detail shops in the immediate area that picks up and delivers cars and comes directly to the customer's home or workplace. Currently, the other shops offer either on-site detailing or mobile detailing. While KRD certainly will provide services to people of all ages, the bulk of the customers are expected to be in the middle- to upper-level income bracket due to the shop's prime location. This is likely to help increase the price point of sale, as many of the prospects in our target market own expensive foreign and domestic vehicles and are more likely to use services more frequently. They also are prime consumers of luxury add-on services like gold trim restoration. Finally, the harsh Chicago winters and rainy springs are likely to contribute to KRD's success. The aforementioned affluent prospects are likely to purchase detailing services that can protect their vehicle from inclement weather and particulates like road salt and acid rain.

## Market Segmentation

Despite specializing in detailing services for luxury vehicles, the prices at KRD will still be reasonable for any budget because of our ability to create customized packages for every customer. Prices per visit will range from $25 for hand-washing to $150 for hand-washing, waxing, and buffing. It is expected that such reasonable rates create a broad base of return customers who will elect to have serviced on a regular schedule. With the variety of services, packages, and products provided to clients, KRD definitely will appeal to people of all ages and incomes.

## Market Analysis

It is expected that about 70 percent of KRD's customer base will come from customers who drop off their vehicle and claim it themselves after the service is completed. Given the local demographics, these customers are most likely to be professional young men and women (aged 20–35), as well as a fair percentage of professional men and women of middle age. The average age of customers in this segment is 33.

Pick-up and delivery service customers are expected to constitute about 15 percent of the customer base. As previously mentioned, these customers will prefer to have one of our professional drivers pick the vehicle up from their home or workplace, take it to the detailing shop for servicing, then return it to the point of origin. We expect average age of customers in this segment to be 45, as they are likely to be full-time people, both executives and salaried employees, who have minimal leisure time. The makeup by gender in this segment is about 75 percent male and 25 percent female.

Another 7 percent of our customer base is likely to use mobile detailing services, where the detail work is performed wherever the vehicle is parked (either at a residence or a workplace). It is our belief that the chief consumers of these services will be men and women aged 45–60, although it is possible that executives and other office-building workers may be amenable to the idea of detailing at their workplace. However, it is our belief that the more upscale the neighborhood or business district, the less likely there will be on-site detailing customers.

Finally, 8 percent of the business for KRD is likely to come from online purchases of either car washing and detailing products or gift items. While younger people often are the most frequent online purchasers because they are comfortable with the technology, we believe that our buyers could come from across the board.

In terms of age, it is expected that the greatest number of users will be among women aged 35–55 because they have more disposable income, yet may not be not willing to do the upkeep necessary on a vehicle themselves. The second-largest group is likely to be men aged 20–34, who will be interested in keeping up appearances through the use of detail-shop services. Because of their active lifestyles, they are most likely to have their cars picked up and delivered to their home or workplace. The smallest market is likely to be composed of women aged 20–34, who are probably more likely to spend their disposable income on their children; and men and women over the age of 55. However, those who are still employed after age 55 may still be prime users. This group offers the greatest potential for growth, which can be achieved by stressing the convenience of having someone else do the work, as well as the necessity of keeping vehicles in peak condition for longer life. Emphasizing how detailing protects vehicles against the elements is another strong selling point.

## Target Market Segment Strategy

To build a strong customer base, KRD will continually search for new ways to connect on a more personal level with customers of every age and gender. A larger customer base would provide a significant increase in sales in every area of the business. While the competing detailing shops in the Chicago area offer some of the same services as our company, none have all the services that we offer, nor do they have an eco-friendly product line.

Advertising will be one of the chief ways we will seek new customers and grow the client base. Previous detailing studies have indicated that point-of-purchase materials, fliers, door hangers, marriage mail, and couponing work better than newspaper advertising, so we will focus our attention there. We also will launch an e-mail newsletter for our clientele, alerting them about shop specials, new products, and more, and we will promote special-event services and our eco-friendly products on an ongoing basis. Other services that will help to increase revenue include the aforementioned pick-up and delivery service, as well as mobile detailing.

Promotion of detailing specials will take place at the Web site and the shop in Chicago, with seasonal detailing being the area of greatest potential.

It is our intention to craft advertising efforts directly and squarely at the more affluent consumers in our target market. Our research has shown that we have a large percentage of luxury vehicle owners in our target market, and they are likely to be interested in detailing services that will pamper and preserve their vehicles.

KRD also will explore social networking media such as Facebook and Twitter as a way to take marketing efforts to a new level. Initially, the target audience for such efforts will be prospects in their 20s; however, research published on iStrategyLabs (**www.istrategylabs.com**), a digital word-of-mouth agency, has shown that 29 percent of Facebook users are in the 35–54 age group, versus 24.8 percent in the 25–34 age group. Therefore, because it is reasonable to assume that the more mature age group will have more discretionary income, we will certainly include them in our Facebook marketing efforts.

While the social networking site Twitter is still in its infancy, it has grown exponentially over the past 18 months and therefore deserves our attention as a potential marketing platform. A 2009 Pew Internet and & American Life Survey indicated that 33 percent of online adults aged 18–29 have used Twitter or another "status update" site, while another 22 percent of online adults aged 30–49 have used it. These are numbers too significant to ignore, so KRD plans to explore the possibilities immediately.

## Competition

As mentioned previously, KRD is situated in an affluent section of the Chicago metropolis that currently is serviced by just one other detailer. That detailer does not specialize, nor does he offer mobile detailing. There are actually hundreds of car washes (many of which offer detailing services) and detailing shops in the Chicago metropolis. While the car washes generally are well-established, having been in business for 8 or more years, the detailers are not, which leads us to believe that our main competition comes from car washes rather than detailers. Because car washes generally do not offer mobile services, we have an automatic advantage in that area that we can exploit through education and advertising. We also have the tremendous benefit of being in an area with higher incomes and higher property values. Well-heeled people are greater consumers of discretionary purchases like detailing services, as are those who own larger, more luxurious vehicles.

## Competitive Edge

As mentioned previously, KRD will enjoy an automatic advantage in the marketplace by offering services like pick-up and delivery services, mobile detailing, and remote appointment booking, In addition, KRD will strive to gain a competitive edge in the market through the education and training of its technician workforce. We aspire to be more than just car washers; we want our technicians to understand everything from paint analysis to product benefits. In addition to arranging for manufacturer reps to give in-house demonstrations, we will constantly look for opportunities to educate our workforce, both through hands-on experiences and formal education. We want our workforce to be professional, proficient, and proud, and investing in their education is a solid way to do that.

This strategy also will lead to a more satisfied workforce. The hope is that a happy workforce will provide better customer service, thus making our clients happy, too, and ultimately making them more likely to return for future service. Toward that end, we will devise an in-house training program for new hires that focuses on the basics of customer service. The result will be a courteous, well-informed workforce that is knowledgeable about customers' vehicles, capable of making intelligent recommendations, and responsive to customers' needs.

## Prospective Financial Data

We believe KRD is perfectly positioned to see steadily increasing revenues over the next five years. While we do expect growth in the first year to be somewhat slower, we anticipate strong growth in two to three years as our reputation grows. We also believe that, with the right advertising, sales of our eco-friendly products should be strong right from the start.

| SALES FORECAST | | | |
|---|---|---|---|
| | FY 2011 | FY 2012 | FY 2013 |
| On-site detailing | $100,000 | $150,000 | $200,000 |
| Mobile detailing | $7,000 | $15,000 | $25,000 |
| Product sales | $10,000 | $12,000 | $14,000 |
| Total sales | $117,000 | $177,000 | $239,000 |

## Funding Specifics

We respectfully request a start-up loan of $150,000. The funds will be used as follows:

1.  Secure and purchase a 5,000-square-foot facility

2.  Renovate the building to accommodate three detailing bays, a 500-square-foot office, and a 1,000-square-foot waiting area

3.  Install sand trap and oil separator (required by the EPA) and connect to the sanitary sewer for disposal of gray water

4.  Purchase two fully equipped mobile detailing rigs

5.  Cover operating expenses for 18 months (equipment, detailing products, personnel, training)

Future funding needs may include up to $25,000 per year for three years for additional research and development of eco-friendly products.

## Appendix

(The Small Business Administration recommends including here additional information like a personal and professional credit history; résumés of key management personnel; letters of reference; copies of necessary licenses, permits, or patents; and a list of professional business consultants, including an attorney and accountant.)

## Back Cover

### Kenneth Russell Detailing
*Details Are Our Business*

### Amount to Secure: $150,000
### September 2011

This document is a business plan and is neither an offer to buy or sell as a solicitation to purchase. This business plan for Kenneth Russell Detailing is confidential and includes certain proprietary information that is considered to be trade secrets for Kenneth Russell Detailing. As such, neither this plan nor any of the information provided herein may be reproduced or disclosed to any person under any circumstances without written permission of Kenneth Russell Detailing.

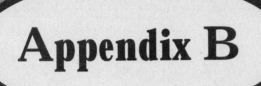

# Appendix B

## Sample Performance Evaluations and Employment Forms

# Sample Performance Evaluation

Name: _____

Job title: _____

Date of evaluation: _____

Date of hire: _____

| EMPLOYEE EVALUATION | |
| --- | --- |
| *Responsibilities* | *Rating* |
| *Performs duties outlined in job description* | *Outstanding Above Meets Below N/A* |
| *Comments:* | |
| | |

| Customer service skills | Outstanding Above Meets Below N/A |
|---|---|
| Comments: | |

| Teamwork | Outstanding Above Meets Below N/A |
|---|---|
| Comments: | |

| Follows directions | Outstanding Above Meets Below N/A |
|---|---|
| Comments: | |

Opportunities for improvement:

Manager signature: _____ Date: _____

Employee signature: _____ Date: _____

# Employment Application Sample

Please complete this job application by printing clearly in black or blue ink and answering all questions. At the end of the form, please sign your name and date the application.

## PERSONAL INFORMATION

Name: _____

Street address: _____

City, state, ZIP code: _____

Phone number: (___)_____

Are you eligible to work in the United States and do you have your proper documents proving eligibility? Yes _____ No_____

If you are under age 18, do you have an employment/age certificate? Yes _____ No _____

Have you been convicted of or pleaded no contest to a felony within the last five years?.
Yes _____ No _____

If yes, please explain: _____
_____
_____

## POSITION/AVAILABILITY

Position you are applying for: _____

Days/hours available for work:
*(Please check each box that is applicable):*

☐ Monday
☐ Tuesday
☐ Wednesday
☐ Thursday
☐ Friday
☐ Saturday
☐ Sunday

Hours available: Morning _____ Afternoon _____ Evenings _____

What date are you available to start work?_____

## EDUCATION

Name and address of school • Degree/diploma • Graduation date:

_____
_____
_____
_____
_____
_____

Skills and qualifications: licenses, skills, training, awards:

_____
_____
_____
_____
_____
_____

## EMPLOYMENT HISTORY

*PRESENT AND LAST POSITION:*

Employer: _____

Address:_____

Supervisor: _____

Phone number: (___)_____

E-mail: _____

Position title: _____

From: _____ To: _____

Responsibilities: _____
_____
_____

_____

_____

Salary: _____

Reason for leaving: _____

_____

*PREVIOUS POSITION:*

Employer: _____

Address:_____

Supervisor: _____

Phone number: (___)_____

E-mail: _____

Position title: _____

From: _____ To: _____

Responsibilities: _____

_____

_____

_____

_____

Salary: _____

Reason for leaving: _____

_____

May we contact your present employer?
Yes _____ No _____

## REFERENCES

Name/title, address, phone:

_____

_____

_____

_____

_____

_____

I certify that information contained in this application is true and complete. I understand that false information may be grounds for not hiring me or for immediate termination of employment at any point in the future if I am hired. I authorize the verification of any or all information listed above.

Signature: _____

Date:_____

# Appendix C

## Market Research Survey

# Market Research Questionnaire

A market research questionnaire is an efficient way to collect useful information about the prospects in your target market area. By asking questions about prospects' previous detailing purchase behavior and future intentions, you can figure out which services might be of most interest to them, as well as how to price them.

It can cost thousands of dollars to have a market research professional create a survey for you. Because you will probably prefer to keep your start-up funds for other purposes, you can write your own survey questions. To help you in the process, here is a list of questions you might consider asking your prospects. You may wish to add other questions that reflect your local demographics or service choices.

## General background questions

What kind of vehicle do you drive?

Make: _____

Model: _____

Year: _____

How long have you owned this vehicle? _____

Have you ever considered having your car professionally detailed?

☐ Yes
☐ No

If not, why not? _____

## Specific detailing questions

If you have your car professionally detailed, how often?

☐ Weekly
☐ Monthly
☐ Annually
☐ Seasonally (spring, fall)
☐ Other (specify) _____
_____

How much do you pay for interior detailing? Exterior detailing? _____
_____

Have you ever used mobile detailing services?

☐ Yes
☐ No

Would you be interested in mobile detailing services at your home or workplace?

☐ Yes
☐ No
☐ Maybe

Which detailing services are most important to you?
(Check all that apply)

    ☐ Hand-wash and vacuum
    ☐ Hand wax
    ☐ Upholstery cleaning/spot removal
    ☐ Carpet cleaning/spot removal
    ☐ Odor removal
    ☐ Dent repair
    ☐ Other

What is the most you would spend for a complete
professional detailing?

    ☐ Under $100
    ☐ $100–$150
    ☐ $151–$200
    ☐ More than $200

Please rank the following factors in terms of their importance to you
with 1 being most important and 5 being least important

Price

*MOST IMPORTANT*    1    2    3    4    5    *LEAST IMPORTANT*

Business hours

1    2    3    4    5

Drop-in service (no appointment needed)

1    2    3    4    5

Quick turnaround time while you wait

1    2    3    4    5

Retail items available for sale

1    2    3    4    5

Mobile detailing

1    2    3    4    5

Excellent customer service

1   2   3   4   5

## Demographic questions

What is your annual household income?

☐ Under $25,000
☐ $25,001–$50,000
☐ $50,001–$75,000
☐ $75,001–$100,000
☐ More than $100,000

What is your profession? _____

What is your age group?

☐ Under 25
☐ 26–39
☐ 40–55
☐ Over 55

# Other factors to consider

To increase the chances of having your surveys returned, keep it to a one-sided page, provide a self-addressed stamped envelope with the survey, and make it optional for respondents to provide their address. However, if you would like to use this marketing effort as a way to start collecting names and addresses for your company mailing list, offer a prize (like a free exterior detailing or a basket of detailing products) and ask for full contact information, including phone number and e-mail address. Also be sure to add a question asking for permission to send promotional information to the prospect in the future.

# Appendix D

## Resources

## Demographics information

| Name | Phone number | Web site |
|------|--------------|----------|
| Buy Demographics | 800-504-1708 | www.buydemographics.com |
| U.S. Census Bureau | 800-923-8282 800-877-8339 | www.census.gov |

## Detailing associations

| Name | Phone number | Web site |
|------|--------------|----------|
| Auto Detailing Network | n/a | www.autodetailingnetwork.com |
| Central States Carwash Association | 888-545-9151 | CSCAcarwashpros@aol.com |
| International Carwash Association | 888-ICA-8422 | www.carwash.org |
| Heartland Carwash Association | 515-224-6845 | www.heartlandcarwash.org |
| Mid-Atlantic Carwash Association | 888-378-9209 | www.mcacarwash.org |
| Midwest Carwash Association | 800-546-9222 | www.midwestcarwash.com |

| New England Car Wash Association | 781-245-7400 | www.newenglandcarwash.org |
| Southeastern Car Wash Association | 800-834-9706 | www.secwa.org |
| Southwest Car Wash Association | 512-343-9023 | www.swcarwash.org |
| Western Carwash Association | 916-235-4135, 800-344-9274 | www.wcwa.org |

## Detailing education

| Name | Phone number | Web site |
| --- | --- | --- |
| Auto Detailing Institute | 570-643-2538 | www.autodetailinginstitute.com |
| Detail in Progress | 619-701-1100 | www.detailinprogress.com |
| Detail King | 888-314-0847 | www.detailking.com |
| Detail Plus Car Appearance Systems | 800-284-0123 | www.detailplus.com |
| The Ding King Inc. | 800-3043464 | www.dingking.com |
| Kleen Car Auto Appearance | 888-302-6400 | www.1car detailing-training.com |
| Rightlook.com | 800-883-3446 | www.rightlook.com |

## Detailing newsletters

- Auto Detailing Network (**www.autodetailingnetwork.com**)
- AutoGeek.net (**www.autogeek.net**)
- Detail City (**www.detailcity.org**)
- Detail King (**www.detailking.com**)

## Detailing Systems

| Name | Web site |
| --- | --- |
| Appearance Plus Inc. | www.appearance-plus.com |
| Detail Plus Car Appearance Systems | www.detailplus.com |
| National Details Systems Inc. | www.nationaldetail.com |
| Rightlook.com | www.rightlook.com |

## Eco-friendly product and equipment suppliers

| Name | Phone number | Web site |
|---|---|---|
| Eco Touch Inc. | 888-375-7970 | http://ecotouch.net |
| Rejuvenate Waterless Car Wash | 877-959-1234 | www.rejuvenateauto.com |
| Green Earth Technologies Inc. | 877-438-4761 | www.getg.com |
| Kleen Car Auto Appearance | 888-302-6400 | www.1car detailing-training.com |
| Pressure Power Systems Inc. (Vacu-Boom) | 336- 996-5585 | www.vacuboom.com |
| Professional Detailing Products | 888-999-7627 661-250-2020 | www.3dproducts.com sales@3dproducts.com |
| Zymöl | 800-999-5563 | www.zymol.com customerservice@zymol.com |

## Equipment and supply vendors

| Name | Phone number | Web site |
|---|---|---|
| Auto Wax Co. Inc. | 800-826-0828 | www.autowaxcompany.com |
| Car Planet Detailing | 610-513-9705 | www.carplanetdetailing.com |
| Chemical Guys Mfg. Co. | 310-678-2838 866-822-3670 | www.chemicalguys.com |
| Daimer Industries | 781-393-4900 800-471-7157 | www.daimer.com |
| Detail Plus Car Appearance Systems | 800-284-0123 | www.detail-plus.com |
| Premium Auto Care | 800-487-3347 | www.premiumautocare.com |
| Therma-Kleen | 630-718-0212 800-999-3120 | www.thermaclean.com steamtk@aol.com |
| Top of the Line Detailing Supplies | 800-533-5743 | www.topoftheline.com |

## Financing Information

Free small-business guide to financing: **www.circlelending.com**

## Franchise opportunities

| Name | Phone number | Web site |
|------|-------------|----------|
| Detail Plus Car Appearance Systems | 800-284-0123 | www.detailplus.com |
| Dr. Vinyl | 800-531-6600 | www.drvinyl.com |
| FranchiseWorks.com | 877-824-4411 | www.franchiseworks.com |
| Sparkle Auto | 866-372-9559 | www.sparkleauto.com |
| Ziebart International Corp. | 800-877-1312 | www.ziebart.com |

## Incorporation information

| Name | Phone number | Web site |
|------|-------------|----------|
| Business Filings Inc. | 800-981-7183 | www.businessfilings.com |
| The Company Corp. | 800-818-6082 | www.incorporate.com |
| Find Legal Forms | 800-959-5899 | www.findlegalforms.com |

## Small-business assistance

| Name | Phone number | Web site |
|------|-------------|----------|
| U.S. Small Business Administration | 800-827-5722 | www.sba.gov |
| Business.gov | n/a | www.business.gov |
| Small Business Development Centers | n/a | www.sbaonline.sba.gov/SBDC |
| American Institute of Small Business | 952-545-7001 | www.aisb.biz |

## Trade shows

| Name | Phone number | Web site |
|------|-------------|----------|
| Car Care World Expo | 888-ICA-8422 | www.carwash.org |
| Midwest Carwash Association Expo | 800-546-9222 | www.midwestcarwash.com |
| Western Carwash Association Annual Convention and Trade Show | 916-235-4135 800-344-9274 | www.wcwa.org |
| Mobile Car Tech Expo | 727-531-7850 | www.mobiletechexpo.com |
| SEMA Auto Show | 909-396-0289 | www.semashow.com, www.sema.org |

## Additional business resources

| Name | Phone number | Web site |
|------|--------------|----------|
| Business Owner's Toolkit | n/a | **www.toolkit.com** |
| Minority Business Development Agency | 888-324-1551 | **www.mbda.gov** |
| U.S. Chamber of Commerce | 800-638-6582 | **www.uschamber.com** |

# Glossary

**Acid rain:** Precipitation (including rain, snow, fog, or hail) that has combined with airborne pollutants such as sulfuric or nitric acids. It can harm a vehicle's finish and glass if not removed promptly.

**Air compressor:** A machine used for powering pneumatic tools.

**Bonnet:** Cover used on orbital buffers for the application of polishes and waxes.

**Brake dust:** Particles ground off the brake pads that are deposited on the braking system and wheels and can damage the wheels' finish if not removed.

**Carnauba wax:** A hard, yellowish-brown wax made from the leaves of the carnauba palm. The highest grade is No. 1 yellow and is favored by detailers.

**Carpet extractor:** Device used to pull shampoo and water from carpeting after cleaning.

**Chamois:** Soft leather or synthetic, leather-like cloth used for drying vehicles.

**Claying:** Process of using a clay bar to remove contaminants from painted surfaces.

**Clear coat:** The clear topcoat of paint applied over the pigmented layer of paint (known as the basecoat).

**Creeper:** Platform with wheels on which a detailer lies in order to slide under a vehicle.

**Cutting pad:** Type of buffing pad for removing moderate swirls and scratches.

**Demographics:** Population characteristics such as age, race, gender, and income level, used to determine a target audience for marketing efforts.

**Detailing clay:** A product used to remove contaminants that are embedded in a vehicle's paint finish.

**DBA:** Acronym for "doing business as," referring to the name adopted by a company in place of the owner's legal name.

**Dressing:** Liquid (either water- or solvent-based) used to clean and shine rubber, plastic, vinyl, and leather.

**Express detailing:** Quickie detailing process usually completed in about 15 to 30 minutes.

**Fogger odor remover:** A chemical odor remover that tackles stubborn odors in or clinging to carpet, leather, vinyl, and velour.

**GEM orbital polisher:** Type of polisher that eliminates swirl marks. Also used to apply wax and sealants.

**Goldplating:** Applying a gold finish to the chrome and stainless steel of a vehicle to give it a custom, upscale look.

**Headliner:** The ceiling liner of a vehicle.

**High-speed buffer:** Device that removes scratches and other imperfections and produces high gloss and deep shine.

**Industrial fallout:** Airborne metal particles that settle on a vehicle's finish, where they become embedded. Emissions from factories, as well as rail dust and brake dust, are examples of industrial fallout.

**Interior dryer:** Device used to speed up both interior and exterior drying.

**Lambo doors:** Vehicle doors that open vertically rather than horizontally.

**Logotype (logo):** A graphic element that identifies a company.

**Merchant account:** An account established with a bank or other payment processor to allow a business to accept credit and debit card payments.

**Mission statement:** A succinct statement encapsulating a business's core purpose and why it exists. Optimally, it is used as a "road map" for future operations.

**OEM:** Acronym for Original Equipment Manufacturer. In the automotive industry, it refers to replacement parts manufactured by the company that made the original parts.

**OSHA:** Occupational Safety and Health Administration. The federal agency responsible for safety and health legislation.

**Overspray:** General name for contaminants such as acid rain, fallout, brake dust, road tar, or bugs that settle on a vehicle's surface and erode the finish if not removed promptly.

**Ozone generator:** Device for permanently removing odors from sources such as cigarette smoke, pets, and rancid or stale food. Also kills mold, mildew, bacteria, and viruses.

**Paintless dent repair (PDR):** Process of removing minor dents and dings from a vehicle. Quite effective on minor body damage such as indentations and creases, door dings, and hail damage, but only if there is no paint damage.

**Point-of-sale (POS) terminal:** Refers to the electronic box used to swipe credit/debit cards and verify that the customer's account is in good standing.

**Pressure washer:** Device that produces water under pressure; used for general washing and degreasing.

**Rail dust:** Airborne metal filings from railroads that can settle on and become embedded in a vehicle's surface. Will cause rust spots if not removed promptly.

**Random orbital polisher:** Type of buffer used to remove scratches and scuffs. Differs from a high-speed buffer because its motion imitates hand buffing. It also is easier to master and easier to use.

**Rotary buffer/polisher:** High-speed buffer used to remove paint imperfections such as deep scratches and swirls.

**Sand trap/oil separator:** Device installed in a sanitary sewer to trap contaminants such as oil before the water is discharged into the sewer for treatment in a wastewater plant.

**Skid-mount wash system:** Self-contained pressure-washer unit used by mobile detailers; it can be bolted down into a truck bed or trailer.

**Sustainability:** A way to meet one's current needs without negatively impacting the ability of subsequent generations to meet their own needs.

**Swirl marks:** Micro-scratches left by wool cutting pads used on a vehicle's clear-coat finish.

**Tire dressing:** Solvent-based product used to condition tires.

**Trade name:** The official name of a business that does not use the full legal name of the owner as part of its name. Cranky Franky Auto Detailing is an example of a trade name.

**Turn rate:** The length of time it takes to detail a vehicle.

**Wastewater-reclamation system:** A system usually consisting of a containment mat that goes under the vehicle being detailed, a vacuum for collecting wastewater, and a holding tank for the water.

**Wet-dry vacuum:** A less powerful and less expensive alternative to a carpet extractor.

# Bibliography

Cook, J.M. (2009) *The Profitable Auto Detail Shop*. Sacramento, CA: Cook Shirey Publications

Detail King (**www.detailking.com**)

Detail Plus Appearance Systems (**www.detailplus.com**)

Drive-N-Style (**www.drivenstyle.com**)

Sandlin, Eileen Figure. (2005) *Start Your Own Automobile Detailing Business*. Newburgh, NY: Entrepreneur Press

Steingold, F.S. (2008) *Legal Guide for Starting & Running a Small Business* (10th ed.) Berkeley, CA: NOLO

# Biography

Eileen Figure Sandlin is an award-winning writer and the author of 16 books, including 15 business start-up books. She has published more than 700 magazine and newspaper articles, as well as thousands of newsletter articles. Her writing specialties are health care, small-business issues, and education. Sandlin holds a master's degree in journalism and is a professor of business communication at a major Midwest university.

# Index

How to open & operate a financially successfu
629.2872 SANDL          **31057011287409**

Sandlin, Eileen Figure. 2/2012
WEST GA REGIONAL LIBRARY SYS